Daily Fare

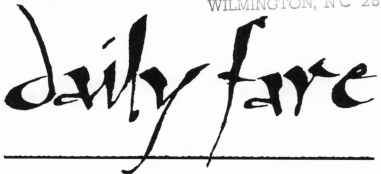

Essays from the
Multicultural Experience

Edited by Kathleen Aguero

The University of Georgia Press Athens and London

© 1993 by the University of Georgia Press
Athens, Georgia 30602
"Black Catholics: Cultural Exiles, Literary Exiles" © 1992 by Yvonne
All rights reserved
Designed by Betty Palmer McDaniel
Set in 10/14 Linotype Walbaum by Tseng Information Systems, Inc.
Printed and bound by Thomson-Shore, Inc.
The paper in this book meets the guidelines for
permanence and durability of the Committee on
Production Guidelines for Book Longevity of the
Council on Library Resources.

Printed in the United States of America

97 96 95 94 93   C   5 4 3 2 1

97 96 95 94 93   P   5 4 3 2 1

Library of Congress Cataloging in Publication Data

Daily fare : essays from the multicultural experience
/ edited by Kathleen Aguero.
p. cm.
Includes bibliographical references.
ISBN 0-8203-1498-6 (alk. paper).
— ISBN 0-8203-1499-4 (pbk. : alk. paper)
1. Pluralism (Social sciences)—United States.
2. United States—Ethnic relations.   3. United States—Race
relations.   I. Aguero, Kathleen.
E184.A1D24   1993   92-15559
305.8'00973—dc20   CIP

British Library Cataloging in Publication Data available

Contents

Preface

As the metaphor of the "melting pot" gives way to that of the "salad bowl," writers in the United States struggle to discover what it means to live in a nation of diverse and competing cultures, to find the balance between merging and preserving traditions, to learn who we are and how to speak and listen to one another. *A Gift of Tongues* and *An Ear to the Ground* explored and celebrated diversity in contemporary United States poetry. In this volume, a variety of American writers describe their experience in the United States today.

Despite the current interest in multiculturalism, the notion of culture in the United States today is too often synonymous with predominantly white, male, heterosexual, upper-class, Eurocentric interests. In compiling this anthology, I invited writers "outside" this dominant tradition to contribute a personal essay. It was important to me to avoid predetermining subject matter or emotional stance by asking for pieces on ethnicity or difference. I wanted the writers to speak freely in order to see what themes would emerge, and so I specified only an essay with a strong first-person point of view, letting this vantage serve as the unifying factor. And yet, despite the variety of essays here—memoirs, analyses, coming-of-age pieces, narratives—common themes *do* emerge, the prevailing one being relationship to culture and the problem of identity. What does "to belong" mean in a multicultural nation where cultures are still ranked and identity is so complex? As Judith Ortiz Cofer learned, "though the Puerto Rican children . . . were often subjected to the scorn and impatience of teachers burdened with too many students making too many demands in a classroom, the blacks were obviously the ones singled out for 'special' treatment." Even within ethnic and racial groups there may be "subgroups." Yvonne speaks of the "buried identity" of black Catholics and others, which lets their experience be ignored. Other writers confront the confusion of a plural heritage. Kiana Davenport, for example, writes, "At the Y with my friends, I tried to hold in my whiteness, but out in the city, I held back my Hawaiian side." This masquerade with its ensuing friendships based on false assumptions prevented "any genuine human contact." The cost of being different and the cost of hiding difference are obviously both high. For Lonny Kaneko, the Japanese-American experience and its problems of acculturation became encapsulated in the image of a Japanese-American man who claimed he lost his thumbs because he didn't eat his breadcrusts: "His example seems to speak that breaking rules, even if the rules aren't clear to everyone, may result in swift emasculation, confinement, and loss of personal rights and dignity"; as a result, he adds, "I've lived my life looking over my shoulder, as if to survey the potential damage I might have carelessly and incautiously caused."

Such obedience necessitates an eternal and inhibiting vigilance. One result may be a complicated and ambivalent relationship to language. English is the language that both empowers and denies, reveals and disguises. For Judith Ortiz Cofer, as a young girl in Paterson, New Jersey, reading gave "a sense of inner freedom, a feeling of power and the ability to fly that is the main reward of the writer." However, Alberto Alvaro Ríos reminds us that although learning English in the first grade meant being able to use "clay, blackboards, cubbyholes, fingerpaint, kickballs that weren't flat," it also meant being punished for speaking Spanish; therefore, "Spanish was bad. Okay. We, then, must be bad kids. So. And our parents still spoke Spanish, our grandparents, and everyone." Mistrust of a language that can hide as well as expose secrets, shame as well as heal, is not peculiar to bilingual speakers. As a child, Minnie Bruce Pratt puzzled over why her family considered some books too dangerous for her to read. Later, in her search for personal truth as a southerner and a lesbian, for the explanations that would clarify her world, she found that some of the answers may have been concealed in the very books which had been forbidden.

All of these writers struggle with censorship and self-censorship, realizing the importance of hearing one another's stories. Those who can speak have an obligation to give voice to the untold stories of their families and communities—the source of daily life, of nourishment and pain. Garrett Hongo is enjoined by Kubota, his grandfather, to hear and retell his story, and Hongo accepts this responsibility as "a ritual payment the young owe their elders who have survived." To support these writers in this charge, to give readers the opportunity to participate in this witnessing, is certainly one of the aims of this collection.

I hope that part of this participation will consist of augmenting, even arguing with, the selection of essays presented here. Clearly this anthology is not meant to be definitive or exhaustive. There are many other stories to be told and many ways of telling them. Rather, these essays honor the possibilities of this point in our history. "We are the hybrids of the new world, making ourselves up as we go along," Kiana Davenport says, and such freedom can be exhilarating as well as burdensome. When Lonny Kaneko writes that "whether one is a rice eater or a bread eater is not so important today. What may be more important is that today we may be neither but a consumer of both," one understands that this tricky balancing act may not only be possible but worth the cost. There is a strong sense of celebration in these essays. The dilemma and the pleasure of such diversity is joyfully summed up in Jack Agüeros's homage to bread: "Ah, Bread, you make me realize that it's hard and wasteful to be purely ethnic in America—definitely wasteful to be totally assimilated." These essays begin to show us that we do not have to choose between being purely ethnic or totally assimilated; that instead we may struggle to pay tribute to our differences and cherish what we have in common without compromising either.

Acknowledgments

These essays previously appeared in various publications.

"The Paterson Public Library," by Judith Ortiz Cofer, appeared in *Witness* (February 1992).

"from *1935*," by Sam Cornish, appeared in *Ploughshares* (Fall 1990) and is excerpted from *1935: A Memoir* (Ploughshares Books). Copyright 1990 by Sam Cornish. Reprinted by permission of the author.

"At an Artists Colony," by Toi Derracotte, appeared in the *Massachusetts Review* (Summer 1988). Reprinted by permission of the author.

"Kubota," by Garrett Hongo, is from *Shining Wisdom of the Law: Japanese Americans and Redress*, by Garrett Hongo, and appeared in a slightly different form in *Ploughshares* (Fall 1990) and in *Best Essays of 1990* (Ticknor and Fields, 1991). Reprinted by permission of the author.

"The Death of Fred Astaire," by Leslie Lawrence, appeared in a slightly different form in the *Colorado Review* (Fall 1992). Reprinted by permission of the author.

"Books in the Closet, in the Attic, Boxes, Secrets," by Minnie Bruce Pratt, appeared in the *American Voice* (Winter 1989) and is included in *Rebellion: Essays 1980–1991* (Ithaca, N.Y.: Firebrand Books, 1991). Reprinted by permission of the author and the publisher.

"Becoming and Breaking: Poet and Poem," by Alberto Alvaro Ríos, appeared in *Ironwood* 24 (Fall 1984). The poem "Nani" is from *Whispering to Fool the Wind* (Sheep Meadow Press). Copyright 1982 by Alberto Ríos. Reprinted by permission of the author.

"Black Hair," by Gary Soto, is from *Living Up the Street*, by permis-

I thank Pine Manor College for a faculty development grant,
which greatly aided work on this collection, Karen Orchard for
her patience, Marie Harris for her continued support and advice even in an "unofficial capacity," and Richard Hoffman for
his encouragement.

Daily Fare

Books in the Closet,
in the Attic, Boxes, Secrets

I

When I was growing up, my bedroom had two narrow closets. One was for my clothes, with high shelves I had to climb on a chair to reach; there I kept my books. The other closet held quilts, blankets, and boxes of books from Papa's house—my grandfather's books. Since I read all the time I was growing up, I was always rummaging around in these closets, and in those in the dining room and in the hall where books were double-shelved, unseen, forgotten by my mother and father. Since I learned that a book I'd found meaningless a year before could interest me later, every six months or so I unpacked the boxes of Papa's books, leafing through the blotched, thin pages of Alexander H. Stephens's *War Between the States*, a copy of the Koran, odd volumes of an edition of Sir Walter Scott's *Works* including *Ivanhoe*, and all of Agnes Strickland's *Lives of the English Queens* in red leatherette binding that rubbed off on my sweaty, eager hands. Mixed in with these books were others more recent, of this century—old grammars, serious best-sellers from the 1930s, and some paperbacks.

One day when I was eleven or twelve, I came upon a paperback I'd set aside many times before, a cheap edition with a picture on the cover in lurid colors, a desperate-looking woman in a white Puritan's cap, the red letter *A* enormous on her breast. It was a book I'd never heard of, but it looked interesting; it looked like a story in which something happened,

I

where there was a secret, something hidden in that letter to be found out.

As I held the book in my hand, my mother came into the room and, looking at the cover, said she didn't want me to read that book, not yet anyway: would I promise her not to read it? Her request was rare, momentous; she was a mother who almost never asked for obedience; and so I agreed.

I know now the book was hardly scandalous. It was *The Scarlet Letter*; by then, 1958, it was over a hundred years old, written about a time three hundred years before, and written in a style that would have been stilted, archaic, to my twentieth-century ears. But my mother did not want me to read this book. What was the secret in it that I was not supposed to know? Was the secret the power of sex? Or the hypocrisy of Christianity, the preacher who taught an ideal and then sneaked off in the woods to do the opposite? Was the secret the vulnerability of a woman alone in the power of a man? Or was the dangerous secret of the story that it revealed the woman's way of thinking, and that of her child? Was the danger of this book, ultimately, that the secret is revealed? That the woman is not left to suffer alone, the frailty of the man is exposed, and the hidden sin, the thing never talked about, the betrayal of love, is confessed? Why was it dangerous for me to read that book?

I didn't think of reading as dangerous; as a child, I read the way people now watch TV or go to the movies. In my tiny Alabama town, Centreville, there was no public library. Across the river, in Brent, there was a one-room collection behind the fire station, for white folks only. The school libraries were all even smaller, and locked up during the summers. Most of the books available to me were in closets, attics, or old mahogany glassed-in bookshelves in a back hall, in the homes of my kin or the middle-class folks who belonged to our church. During the long, burning summer I would ride my bike to Robert and Laura Belle's, or to Miz Gwen Kennedy's, or walk down to my Uncle Francis's house, having gotten permission to borrow books any time I wanted. I'd go into the cool hallway or inner porch, through doors that were never locked, to prowl in the shelves and boxes, looking, looking.

What was I looking for, as I sat in my uncle's attic, sorting through boxes of books, hundreds of paperbacks bought at the drugstore, mysteries, westerns, historical romances, dusty crumbly yellow paper, alluring covers? Perhaps I was hunting for escape, some secret hidden in the books about how to get away from this town, my life. I began to read the way the men in my family drank—my father, his brothers—to escape. Sitting in the attic, poring over the cheap hidden books, I felt the intense excitement of their secret: a way to leave behind life as we were living it, which was so sad and unalterable.

And perhaps I was looking for an explanation. The only answer that I'd ever been given for my life was the Bible, the book that told what the past was, what the future would be. This was the only true story, from creation to judgment day, heaven, hell, and everything in between. What was written in the Bible (the King James version) was the literal truth, not to be questioned, the truth that justified the world as it was, from who owned the sawmill to who drove the log trucks, from why Black people lived in the quarters to why we lived on the hill. The only explanation for how I lived was that it had been so ordered by God, and disclosed by the words of his Book.

The other books I found, searching around town, were almost all stories that existed within this preordained boundary. There was my favorite girls' series, the one I saved my allowance to buy, about the Little Colonel, a granddaughter of the old Confederacy, white, rich, who had house parties, boarding-school escapades. There were the nineteenth-century romances by Augusta Evans Wilson, *The Speckled Bird, St. Elmo*, in which brilliant, intellectual, poor white heroines surrender in Christian love and move up in class status by marrying the rakish, wealthy, but ultimately reformed, white hero. There was Tennyson, and Margaret Mitchell's *Gone with the Wind*. All lying fictions that distorted history and justified the old patterns of white over Black, money over poverty, man over woman.

Of lesbian and gay existence I read not a word, except for a passage in Dante's *Inferno*, an old translation from the Harvard Five-Foot Shelf of Books found at an uncle's. It was a translation I read with fascination but little comprehension, not knowing what most of the sins people were being punished for *were*, but relishing the punishments, the mesmerizing descriptions, never really understanding what the sodomites of the Third Round of the Seventh Circle had done.

I spent hours, days, years reading, trying to ignore the fearfulness and uncertainty of my own life; a life I lived, without understanding, in the midst of the anxious contradictions of huge secrets. In a town where people publicly preached that Blacks were close to inhuman, even animal, I was being raised by a Black woman; in a town in which white men prided themselves on protecting their women, at home it was clear that my father could barely change a light bulb or keep his checking account in order, and that my mother was the economic mainstay of our family; in a town in which people emphasized that they treated all others as *individuals*, in high school we all knew who would definitely go on to college, and who wouldn't, out of our graduating class of sixty-six people.

None of these hidden contradictions to the public story was ever talked about in the town—that I heard—or written about in the books I read. I continued to escape into romances— Shakespeare, Jane Austen, the Brontës, Book-of-the-Month Club excerpts from popular novels—all the same old story. If about a man, it was his fight with the monster, the god, or nature, some kind of puzzle, some kind of trial; if he won, his reward at the end was Heaven, the kingdom, or the girl. If about a woman, the story told of her being good, maybe even a little smart, and waiting for the man to kiss her.

I read the same plot over and over, and found no explanation for why things were the way they were. I found no escape from my life except through fantasy, the thrill of passivity, blotting out my actual life by reading the repetitious fictions, trying to convince myself of the beginning, middle, and end. But two or three times I chanced on a book that gave me a glimpse of other possibilities.

I found an odd volume of Proust, a fragment of *Remembrance of Things Past*, on an aunt's bookshelf next to Gene Stratton-Porter. It was the volume with the passage (famous to others, but marvelous and unknown to me) in which the narrator dips a *madeleine* into fragrant tea, and, eating it, by taste and scent remembers a place, re-creates a village entire from his past. There I glimpsed how the imagination might do more than escape through fantasy; there I glimpsed how I might be able to stand apart from myself while in myself, and meditate on where I lived and who I was.

In the attic I uncovered a copy of *Lady Chatterley's Lover*, which I had to sneak home because by then I was fourteen, and my cousin Andrea, who sat all day in the living room near the bottom of the attic stairs, was checking to see what books I might be finding with sex in them. It was the edition of Lawrence's novel with an introduction that reviewed court decisions on the banning of the book, and that justified the publication of this writing, which certainly was condemned to be a dirty secret in my town. In this I heard not so much the sexual murmurs of the fiction, which were merely more explicit words for what I'd been reading all along. The galvanizing voice was that of the introduction, my first hearing of a contradictory voice, an argumentative voice, one that said that *anything* can be talked about, any secret, a voice that gave me my first belief that what is hidden could be told.

But in the one rickety bookcase in our house there was a book I looked at and never read, a copy of Lillian Smith's *Strange Fruit*, that novel about secret love, the most forbidden book of the modern South. Perhaps I didn't read it because I couldn't take it from the shelf for long without my mother knowing. Perhaps because I glanced through it and was too afraid of what might leap from its pages—the stark punishments for love, and the belief that love could exist across the barrier of Black and white, and, therefore, across all barriers. Indeed, although I couldn't know this then, Smith portrayed not just a love affair between a white man and a Black woman but also, briefly, troublingly, a relationship between two women. Why didn't I read Lillian Smith's novel, which sat quietly, openly, on the bookshelf in my own house, where I had read and reread almost every other book? Perhaps because with a glance at even one of the pages I knew she was going to tell the secrets behind a story that was happening not three hundred years ago but at that moment, near me. Perhaps because the book was only one voice, and there was no other. Perhaps because the only voices I'd heard—the preacher, the governor, other politicians, my teachers, my father—all said the opposite of this one book; and the romances I'd read said there was only one story that had a happy ending. It was too dangerous to pick up and read that book and be alone with the secret: that there was another way to live. And how *could* there be a book written by a human being that contradicted the Bible? If I opened that book, chaos would fly out. I needed a guide through chaos before I was ready to give up predictable romance and distorted history and the literal word of the Bible and everything in my town that was justified by those words, before I was ready for a different kind of book, a different way to live in the world.

In the years after I went off to college at the University of Alabama, I never heard Lillian Smith's name, though we were in the heart of the civil rights years, though people were being shot and blown up all around me, though she was the white southern writer who delved most deeply into the secrets of my region and my life. I wasn't taught her work, or that of Dr. King, or any other literature of liberation. Instead, the writers admired by me and the other students I consorted with were the Fugitives, who flourished at Vanderbilt from 1922 to 1928, white southern men, some of whom later went on to establish the groups known as the Agrarians and the New Critics. Of them Smith said: "No writers in literary history have failed their region as completely as they did."[1]

Indeed, they failed me. I was taught by men who had studied under the Fugitives and by men who shared their beliefs, their literary sons, who handed down their values about writing and its relation to life. And these values were those of my father: love of the land and denial of those who had done the work on the land, despair and belief in death, a fascination with the past of the old heroes, a failure to understand the new heroes and heroines who were liberating the present.

But the Fugitives wrote the old values so eloquently, so elegantly. I, who had heard the values of the white South articulated only in the furious ravings of my father, in the vitriolic demagoguery of George Wallace, and in the sentimental prose of romances, luxuriated in the beauty of language and the ironic detachment of these writers. I was happy to let them express my relationship to my region, as John Crowe Ransom did in his "Antique Harvesters." I had no understanding of how my identity as a white woman was bound to the idea in his lines on the South as the famous Lady, "the Proud Lady, of the heart of fire, / The look of snow." I had no understanding of the history of lynching, murder, rape against Black folks by white men that was justified and excused by the myth of pure white southern womanhood.[2]

When my husband wanted me to name our first child, a

son, Ransom, I agreed. I didn't understand that my husband—whose family was not from the southern elite, but rather small shopkeepers, car salesmen, career military—was trying with our son's name to take a place within the long history of white male rule in the South. That through this naming he would live out some fantasy of being among the elite, among the poets who were still "fighting in retreat" for the Confederacy, fighting for "the land we dreamed to save."[5]

The time of my marriage and early motherhood was a time when Vietnam shriveled beneath defoliants and the people of Vietnam burned with napalm; and the streets of Washington, Chicago, Pittsburgh burned after the assassination of Martin Luther King, Jr. I, and my husband, and our friends John Finlay and Rette Maddox, and most of the other young writers I knew, turned away from this burning landscape. Like other writers all over the country, we lived out the heritage of the Fugitives, turning away from the cruel, fertile present to retreat into a tidy boxed structure of words. We bent ourselves to a closer and closer examination of words, making of writing a world in itself, applying what we understood of the New Criticism by escaping into art, into the story, into the poem. We shut out the feelings, thoughts, and histories of people who lived in other dimensions of the world than ours; we shut ourselves up, solitary, with our art.

From the Fugitives, the closest comment on what was happening around us in the 1960s were some lines of Allen Tate's at the end of "The Swimmers," his poem about how a child meets up with a lynch mob and how the child follows the corpse being dragged back into town:

I could not run
Or walk, but stood. Alone in the public clearing
This private thing was owned by all the town,
Though never claimed by us within my hearing.

With a momentary flash, Tate finally reveals one of the secrets; he claims that murdered body, he announces or confesses the sin. Yet at the same time he denies the humanity and the life of the Black man killed by white men: "This private thing." In the chaos of those days, I had this flash from Tate but no more, nothing else to go on.[4] In a continuation of this silence, there was no sustained public discussion by my teachers or my classmates about the contemporary challenge to the supremacy of white men in the South—to their social system, their economic system, to the way in which everything, especially love between people, had been rigidly ordered by them.

Of the name *Fugitive*, Ransom had said, "It seemed to be a secret among us, though no one knew what the secret was."[5] Sidney Hirsch, who was Jewish and a member of the original group, named them *Fugitives*. But there were no poems from him explaining his meaning of that need to escape. Instead, Tate appropriated his point of view by writing: "A Fugitive was quite simply a Poet: the Wanderer, or even the Wandering Jew, the Outcast, the man who carries the secret wisdom of the world."[6] Of course, Tate and Ransom, Davidson and Penn Warren, and others of the group, white and Christian, were never outcast. They became the literary establishment; they collected Guggenheims, Bollingers, Pulitzers, by writing as refugees from a pastoral communal golden South that had never existed.[7] They perpetuated this self-delusive romance, this glorification of the old hierarchy, as "secret wisdom." Of the buried lives of the South, the secrets from which they fled, there was no word from them, at least not within my hearing.

2

The house that I've just moved to has an attic, which is where I work, read, and write. Every day as I climb up the narrow angle-twisted stairs, I feel the rush of anticipation that I used to feel when I climbed up into somebody's attic to find a new book: going up to a secret place, a hideout, away from the grown-ups. Now I shiver with anticipation and also some fear, because what I mostly do up in this attic is to write about the secret between me and the world, my lesbian self. The secret is myself, and I'm going up, not to escape her, but to meet her.

My attic is lined with rows of books, and boxes of them sit around, not yet unpacked, books about all sorts of folks, especially lesbians, books with startling titles and lurid covers, the kind a mother might snatch from a daughter's hand, books that might provoke a discussion between two women sharing a house and a bedroom when, just before family is to come for a visit, they debate if the books should be moved to a higher shelf, if they should be boxed up and put in the closet.

It's true our books give our secrets away. During the time that I was falling in love with another woman and coming out as a lesbian, my mother arrived for a visit. I had her stay in my tiny bedroom-study, and left my books out as they were, *Lesbian Nation* stacked on top of *Sisterhood Is Powerful*, clues about who I was becoming. Now, years later, strange as it seems, I am someone who writes such books. I've been imagining with satisfaction how my next book of poetry, *Crime Against Nature*, will be the subject of debates on whether it should be hidden, as the kind of book a visitor, browsing in the shelves, would immediately pull down in order to see what secrets it discloses.

Breaking silence/coming out/becoming visible/speaking out: all themes common not just to me but to much of contemporary lesbian writing.[8] Certainly this emphasis is to be expected in a literature springing from our experience: in order to live fully as lesbians we have to be able to *find* each other. And since we don't grow up grouped together as a people by skin color or religion or family; since, despite all the stereotypes, there is, in fact, no way to identify a lesbian just by looking at her; we have to make ourselves known to one another somehow, by glance, by code, by words.

But I didn't find myself as a writer, or as a lesbian, or as a person who had something to say because of words that I read in a book. During the years of my so-called education, both undergraduate and graduate, I continued to escape my daily life as a wife and mother by reading books into which I could flee as an imaginary participant. I also perfected the kind of escape I had learned from the Fugitives and the New Critics: I stood back and looked at literature as an artifact to be commented on; I learned to build my own closed space as a critic by constructing narrow theories about what I read. Even when writing was clearly immediate and present, as, for instance, a poem my husband was writing about me, I still refused to see the words as connected to my life. I accepted Tate's pronouncement of a poem as a thing of "perfect inutility."[9] I managed to forget that, in the year before I married, I, briefly, wrote poetry. I remained trapped in someone else's version of my life; I existed as if I were reading my own life as a badly written novel, which I called "reality."

My ability to imagine another reality for myself came not from something that I read but from meeting up with people who were living a hidden reality out in the open. I met a group of women in the small southern university town where I was in graduate school, a group of women emerging in the Second Wave of Women's Liberation during the 1970s in the United States. With them came *talk*, the subversive talk of one woman with another, me talking to the women who were like me but different, my other selves.

That there was a connection between hidden life and literature was something I glimpsed when I began having conversations with another graduate student, Elizabeth, a feminist who had been very kind to me during the time of my second pregnancy. One day, during lunch, I recounted to her something that had occurred in the class I'd taught that morning on Chaucer's *Canterbury Tales*. I had made a joke about the Pardoner, who is described as having long, yellow, shoulder-length hair and a high voice "like a goat"; he is beardless and never shaves; Chaucer declares him either "a gelding or a mare," either a eunuch or a queer.[10]

Suddenly, in the middle of joking to the class, I wondered if there were any gay men or women there at that moment, enduring this humiliation from me. And as I talked to Elizabeth I remembered, and mentioned, that I had learned this joke from my husband, who used it in his teaching, and who had learned it from what teacher of his? I was mouthing his words like a ventriloquist's dummy.

When I finished this story, Elizabeth looked at me and said with some hesitation, "I should tell you that I am having a relationship with Linda." She did not, at that moment, use the word *lesbian*, but we both heard it resonate in the room. This was the first time I heard one of the hidden truths spoken, not as they had been, in whispers, one person gossiping to another about *someone else*, voyeuristic talk, but, instead, the secret truth spoken to me by the one living this truth, someone outside boxed-in life as I had known it, outside literature as I had learned it. I was suddenly, momentarily, on the outside thinking, "Anything can be said, anything can be done," and I meant, "In my life."

From my journal at that time (which I began writing in, because of these conversations, after long years of silence), I noted of myself in relation to my husband: "Fear to question M.—façade will fold, crash—real hatred, fear, despair underneath. I, of course, deeply silent—fear." Of my talks with Elizabeth: "Why am I friends with Elizabeth?—I feel she is honest with me—and cares about me—even if that feeling is only a principled one toward women—but is friendship with her a retreat from reality? I am spending *too much time* with Elizabeth."

But I was spending time not in unreality but in another reality, where there was another way to look at my life. My husband and I had dinner with Elizabeth and her feminist housemate: "M. saying tactless male things while trying to be conciliatory—strain—his assumptions bristled at—I have ignored these assumptions or accepted them—it's almost as hard to see your husband as others see him as it is to see yourself."

But seeing with lesbian eyes, I managed to separate myself from my husband. I began the process of contradicting the plots of all the romances I'd read. Instead of merging my perspective, my thoughts, and my feelings with the hero, instead of waiting around for him to do something, I began to live as myself, as some unknown heroine in some unknown story. Even in my journals I began to sound like I was talking to and for myself, and not like I had been writing to impress someone who might overhear me, some god I had to convince. I began to summon up my life in myself, a new world, through this writing.

I was able to do this because I was not alone. I knew that there were other women to talk to, and there was more than one book to read. There was the enticing sound of one woman talking to another, conversations that went beyond Virginia Woolf's imagination of a book with the sentences "Chloe liked Olivia. They shared a laboratory together . . ."[11] Because Elizabeth had read Isabel Miller's *Patience and Sarah* and recommended it, I read it too. It was my first lesbian book, a historical romance in which I overheard the heroines during their lovemaking, their quarrels, and their discussions about work and money. Elaine gave me Judy Grahn's *Common Woman* poems; Starling gave me Audre Lorde's *New York Head Shop and Museum*. In these poems I heard the voices of women who had not been present at all in the literature I'd been taught, women who were present in my life but not acknowledged by me, poor white women, Black women, women passionately loving other women. Someone told me about June Arnold's *The Cook and the Carpenter* and *Sister Gin*, and about Bertha Harris's *Lover*, all quintessentially lesbian novels by women born and raised in the South, who came to North Carolina and talked during those years about their writing, their politics, and their loves.[12]

I began to want to hear *all* the hidden conversations, all the writings that defied the prearranged endings of heaven or hell based on gender or race or class or who we loved. I was able to find many of these voices because political movements in the United States have nourished subversive traditions of literature—the movements for abolition of slavery, for suffrage and women's rights, the trade union movement for working people, the civil rights movement, the efforts of people who had come to this country as slaves or as immigrants to honor themselves and their people, the efforts of women to honor ourselves. All these movements engendered narratives of liberation, community schools to teach literacy and history, small publishing houses and newspapers, self-published authors, independent bookstores, many stubborn efforts by oppressed peoples.

The feminist and lesbian movement into which I came out had this subversive tradition embodied in hundreds of national, regional, and community newspapers and newsletters, like the monthly mimeographed newsletter Elizabeth and others began, and I helped with briefly, which was eventually given the name *Feminary*. Some years later, Mab Segrest, Susan Ballinger, and others, including me, turned *Feminary* into a regional southern journal for lesbians. We used to joke about how we were the revolutionary answer to the Fugitives, a new literary tradition bent on turning the old values of the South topsy-turvy, a tradition we did our best to create during the years of the magazine, 1978 to 1983.

We were inspired in our effort by the work of other lesbi-

ans determined to create a subversive transformative literature. From 1976 to 1978, Harriet Ellenberger Desmoines and
Catherine Nicholson edited a national lesbian journal, *Sinis-
ter Wisdom*, out of their home in Charlotte, North Carolina.
There were early lesbian and feminist publishing houses, like
Parke Bowman and June Arnold's Daughters, Inc. Though at
that time there were no women's or gay bookstores in North
Carolina, where I was living, I'd buy books at conferences; and
on my way home to Alabama during the summer to see my
mother, I'd go through Atlanta and stop by Charis Books, the
first women's bookstore I ever set foot in. It was shocking to
me that the bookstore was on Moreland Avenue with all the
other stores, two rooms about the size of my high school library,
but with more books, and such books, the likes of which I'd
never seen. Books that had come out of the movement, just as
I had, because of the stories that needed to be told, the forbidden, tender, extreme, bloody, beautiful, life-and-death stories,
springing from just such conversations begun by me and Elizabeth, talking on our lunch hour, sitting in a small, boxy office,
talking back and forth, talking.

3

Sitting up here in my attic now, in the middle of an April
thunderstorm, books stacked all around, I still find it hard to be
the one who writes the books instead of someone who just hides
out up here reading them. I still fall into the trap of despair,
of acquiescence in the predictable ending, and find myself escaping into the comfortable dead end of murder mysteries or
into the easy fantasies of science fiction. I still struggle to live
and to write the open-ended, ever-changing story, a prose and
a poetry that is merely, simply, true to the complexity of my
own life.

Despite my skills learned at the university, I would not be

writing now except for the talk among women, among sup-
pressed peoples; talk that has yet to receive its due as part of
culture and of art. I would not be writing now except for the
stubborn underground culture and the political work of lesbians, how we meet and talk in the safety of our homes, in our
bars, in our self-help groups; how we talk, sometimes, of our
lives at public meetings of women; and how, sometimes, we
go out into the world and demand of others that our lives be
recognized.

One of the few regrets of my life is from a time when I was
doing political organizing in North Carolina, and had helped
bring together the first gathering of lesbians, as lesbians, outside the bar in my right-wing, military-base town. When that
small group of women finally sat down together in the den of
the house I shared with two other women, I was thrilled that
they were there—and I didn't listen to a thing they were saying.
I thought that I knew what we should be *doing*, and impatiently
thought about how I would instruct them in this plan all the
while they spoke. And so I did not listen to the Latina who
taught Spanish as a second language in the elementary schools
and was closeted; or to the two red-cheeked flannel-shirt self-
sufficient white dykes who'd just moved down from Alaska and
told everyone they were lesbians; or to the two quiet, cropped-
hair dykes who were in the army and worried about the military
police and confidentiality; or to the physical education teacher
at the local church college who was so terrified to be there that
she got drunk and threw up the entire time the meeting went
on. I didn't listen to them, or to the dyke who was a butcher,
or to the one who was a social worker, or to the one whose
political work had been with the SPCA, and not with battered
women. I didn't listen, really, to any of them, so intent was I
on my own way; and now I bitterly regret this.

Now I know that in order to keep hoping, and living, and
writing, I need work from other women that is rooted in the

messy complexity of our daily lives, work in which we upset the predictable ending. I need all the voices of the women who have been destined for despisal, anonymity, or death, but who have defied, survived, and lived to tell their triumph.[13]

When I last went home to Alabama to speak and read my poetry, to a town just south of Nashville and Vanderbilt, I stood in a room glowing with candles and flowers, in front of an audience gathered together by a small group of lesbians then organizing in the town. I watched one young woman in particular in the audience, her transfigured face, her lips murmuring along with my words. Later, she told me that her throat ached and almost closed as the words came up in her, words that meant so much to her, about loving another woman, passionately.

I like to think that the muscles in her throat were strengthened and made more flexible by her murmuring; that her voice is stronger now; because I need her to tell about her life to me, and to others. Eileen, do you hear? Don't just listen to me and my talking. I need you to tell your own story. And Susan, who was there that night also, I want you to let the world know the power of your voice, which was strong enough to bring someone back from the edge of insanity. And the woman whose name I don't remember—you'd just been fired from your job for being a lesbian—everyone should know how you are driving that bus full of problem children, mostly boys, now, and how you've made the seat behind you the place where any child can sit who's had a bad day, so they can talk it over with you, and how the problem children are not problems on *your* bus anymore. I want everyone to know the power of your voice talking to the world, and I want to know what happens next in your remarkable life.

And I know you've already lost one job (or perhaps your children, your friends, or your family, depending on who you are) because you said you were a lesbian; I haven't forgotten. But you are with the other women there in your town, and all over; we have each other. We know the power of announcing a secret to the world, how word travels fast, and how this is what we fear. But we know also that this is our power.

Notes

1. Lillian Smith, *Killers of the Dream* (New York: Anchor/Doubleday, 1963), p. 199. Michelle Cliff has edited an excellent collection of articles and speeches by Smith, *The Winner Names the Age* (New York: W. W. Norton, 1978).

2. A brief selection of Ransom's work can be found in *The Fugitive Poets*, ed. William Pratt (New York: E. P. Dutton, 1965). For some information on the lynching of Black men, the rape of Black women, and the cult of white womanhood, see Ida B. Wells's autobiography, *Crusade for Justice*, edited by her daughter, Alfreda M. Duster (Chicago: University of Chicago Press, 1970); and Jacquelyn Dowd Halls, *Revolt Against Chivalry* (New York: Columbia University Press, 1979).

3. From Donald Davidson, "Lines Written for Allen Tate on His Sixtieth Anniversary," in Pratt, *The Fugitive Poets*.

4. "The Swimmers," in ibid.

5. *The Fugitives Reunion*, ed. R. R. Purdy (Nashville: Vanderbilt University Press, 1959), p. 122.

6. Pratt, *The Fugitive Poets*, pp. 34–39.

7. For more on the Fugitives in relation to southern literature, see Mab Segrest, "Lines I Dare: Southern Lesbian Writing," in *My Mama's Dead Squirrel: Lesbian Essays on Southern Culture* (Ithaca, N.Y.: Firebrand Press, 1985).

8. For more on these themes, see Bonnie Zimmerman, "The Politics of Transliteration: Lesbian Personal Narratives," in *The Lesbian Issue: Essays from Signs* (Chicago: University of Chicago Press, 1985); and Audre Lorde, "The Transformation of Silence into Language and Action," in *Sister Outsider* (Trumansburg, N.Y.: The Crossing Press, 1984).

9. Tate, quoted in Segrest, *My Mama's Dead Squirrel*, p. 112.

10. Geoffrey Chaucer, *Works*, ed. F. N. Robinson (Cambridge: Riverside Press, 1961), p. 23.

11. Virginia Woolf, *A Room of One's Own* (New York: Harcourt Brace Jovanovich, 1957), p. 87.

12. For bibliographic information about contemporary lesbian literature, see Margaret Cruikshank, *Lesbian Studies* (Old Westbury, N.Y.: The Feminist Press, 1982).

13. I think here especially of Dorothy Allison's recent book of short stories, *Trash* (Ithaca, N.Y.: Firebrand Press, 1988), and her preface, "Deciding to Live."

Becoming and Breaking:
Poet and Poem

I

Maybe 1971 it was, summer, inside my parents' house, in Nogales, on the Arizona border with Mexico. I was doing one day what many, if not all, my friends were: filling out preregistration forms—a recent innovation—for my second year at the University of Arizona. I had two spots left to fill. I was a political science major, but only because my adviser taught it. Yet I did have a focus, a purpose: I spent the entire day thumbing through the catalog for the two easiest courses I could find.

And I found them. Thinking "these are for me," I signed up for first-level classes in poetry writing and fiction writing. How hard could these be? And they were not hard, they were what I was looking for exactly, they were the mythical "easy classes." At least in the beginning.

Then something happened, a small moment, issuing almost from a single phrase. Up to now I had done well in school, and in making the transition to college; though I was the first in my family to go, I didn't have to make many adjustments. The formula was not magic—one simply had to follow through. If someone asked me a question about astronomy, I went to an astronomy book. If a teacher asked me about biology, I went to a different biology teacher and asked. If a report was called for, I went to the encyclopedia and copied it. Like that, school. I could play this.

But the rules changed midstream, and I was unprepared—which, in retrospect, means entirely ready. After the first two or three weeks in these easy classes, getting the jargon and the cool and the rules on spelling, I was asked almost simultaneously in both classes to now *go write one*. A poem. A prose sketch.

There was no reference book, no biology teacher. I could copy things down, of course, but both teachers had expressed thoughts on that ahead of time. There was no place to go. At that moment, school changed for me—and life, if I may be so dramatic. School had always come *at* me; I was the back wall to a tennis player, and I simply let things bounce back. But now, for the first time, school would have to come *from* me, from the inside. From the flick of my wrist, my racquet.

I rebelled, of course, sure I had missed out on some technique along the way, a certain knack, a locker room secret; surely there was some way around this. My first efforts were a kind of treading water, waiting for help. I wrote things never earlier than the night before and often in a Spanish mix so as not to be so easily understood. Buying time. And it worked.

It worked in the sense that no real time could be bought. The more I wrote, the more I realized I had been writing almost all my life—I simply had had no name for it. To get away from schoolwork, I had always written things in the backs of my notebooks. Words, phrases, *things*. Not stories. And certainly not poems; I knew better. The town was hard, and people who wrote were called names, especially if they were guys. And especially if they wrote *poems*. Not me. I kept it hidden, called it nothing, and didn't tell anyone about it. You know, smart.

2

I was born in Nogales, on the border of Mexico. My father is from Tapachula, Chiapas, Mexico, and my mother from Warrington, Lancashire, England. I grew up around my father's family but I look like my mother, which means I got to see two worlds from the beginning, and could even physically experience the difference growing up where I did: I could put, every day of my life, one foot in Mexico and one foot in the United States, at the same time.

Growing up around my father's family and in that town, for all practical purposes my first language was Spanish. My mother, who was the only one who spoke English entirely, was ignored by everyone; not on purpose, but because no one knew what else to do with her. I joke about this, and I must have been learning English, but it is the Spanish I remember hearing.

There was no problem with this until first grade. That little kids can't make some very big decisions is not true. When we got to that first-grade classroom, my friends and I, we were told: you can't speak Spanish. That was crazy, of course, and we all raised our hands, saying *seguro que sí*, "we can, yes." But no: Spanish is bad, don't speak it here. "Bad" was perhaps an unfortunate word choice, but this was a strange time in educational history, and I believe that hearts were in the right place, even if methods weren't. We got swats for speaking Spanish, even on the playground. As children, we had a choice right then. One gets swatted for doing something bad— certainly our parents had taught us that. So if we got swatted for speaking Spanish, Spanish must be bad. This was the bargain, and here was the other side: what we saw when we got to that first-grade classroom was clay, blackboards, cubbyholes, fingerpaints, kickballs that weren't flat. And when we got home that day, we looked around—and didn't see any of that stuff. The decision was easy. We knew what we wanted. And if learning English was going to do it, we weren't dumb, we could go along.

But we learned something else in the bargain of these games. If we spoke Spanish and got swatted for that, Spanish was bad. Okay. We, then, must be bad kids. So. And our parents still spoke Spanish, our grandparents, and everyone. They, then, must be bad people. This was easy enough; we learned to be ashamed of them. We loved them, but we knew the truth. We had no PTA meetings—none of us ever took notes home. By the time I was in junior high school and the beginning of high school, I could no longer speak Spanish—which is to say, I didn't want to, I was embarrassed, and I didn't practice. Not until my later years of high school and college did I relearn Spanish, but that is what I had to do, relearn. It was more than words.

Things have changed since then. I know they have in my hometown. But here is a poem about that time, when I couldn't, or wouldn't, speak Spanish.

I was still going to my grandmother's house once a week at least for lunch, always meatballs with mint from the garden, and she did not then and still does not speak English. What we had to do, essentially, is invent for ourselves, so that neither one of us would suffer, a third language, one that was all our own. Pablo Neruda spoke often about this. We came up with something many will understand. It was simple and it worked. Our language was this, the language of grandmother and grandson: she would cook and I would eat. In this way, with love, we talked. The poem is "Nani," our name, as grandchildren, for her—different from the Refugio, or Doña Cuca, or la Señora de Ríos, that older people used.

Sitting at her table, she serves
the sopa de arroz to me
instinctively, and I watch her,
the absolute *mamá*, and eat words
I might have had to say more
out of embarrassment. To speak,
now-foreign words I used to speak,
too, dribble down her mouth as she serves
me *albóndigas*. No more

than a third are easy to me.
By the stove she does something with words
and looks at me only with her
back. I am full. I tell her
I taste the mint, and watch her speak
smiles at the stove. All my words
make her smile. Nani never serves
herself, she only watches me
with her skin, her hair. I ask for more.

I watch the *mamá* warming more
tortillas for me. I watch her
fingers in the flame for me.
Near her mouth, I see a wrinkle speak
of a man whose body serves
the ants like she serves me, then more words
from more wrinkles about children, words
about this and that, flowing more
easily from these other mouths. Each serves
as a tremendous string around her,
holding her together. They speak
Nani was this and that to me
and I wonder just how much of me
will die with her, what were the words
I could have been, was. Her insides speak
through a hundred wrinkles, now, more
than she can bear, steel around her,
shouting, then, What is this thing she serves?

She asks if I want more.
I own no words to stop her.
Even before I speak, she serves.

3

I wrote the poem in the early 1970s, and by the late 1970s I was doing a good deal of work in the Arizona Artists-in-Education Program, traveling all over the state. As an offshoot and partner to that program, founding the Central Arizona College Community Writing Project, in 1980 I did a week-long residency in Florence, a small town in the middle of the state, not unlike my hometown.

I did the residency as I normally do, giving students a range of exercises, interchange, anecdote. On Friday I read some works of my own, a number of poems, beginning with "Nani" and the story of its making. The event passed simply enough.

The next year I did a second residency in Florence. Friday came and I had decided to again read some of my own work. I jokingly asked if anyone had any requests. A young Mexican girl in the back of the class who had not said a word all week raised her hand.

"Yes?"

"Read the poem you read last year, the one about your grandmother, Nani."

In one sentence she remembered that I had been to the school before, remembered the subject matter of a poem, and remembered its title. Florence, Arizona. A Friday. Hot outside, late September just after my birthday, with the sounds of setting up for a football game later that evening. *I could not remember her name.*

4

"Nani" is not the first poem I wrote, nor the best. But it is the first important one in that the words were important to someone else, this before other things. Someone like me, in a town like mine, a place where no one came to talk about writing poems and what literature could be. I had written, in essence, the first poem to myself.

I would not learn these things about the poem until many years later, of course, not learn that it was a breakthrough poem until long after, when it was no longer breaking through. Yet I knew it was different when I wrote it: more work, more than I had done on anything up to that point. And it came from the inside, the new book. The work was on things I knew, so it wasn't a real kind of work at all. It was, instead, if not a game, a kind of earnest demand, finally, from somewhere inside. I had a story, a real story, for the first time, no fooling around, and I wanted someone else to know it, and sonofagun best of all there it was in front of me all the time. And wasn't this easy, and wasn't life good once again now that I'd found the answer?

Except that it didn't work, not right away and not like I expected. I could not be accurate in the telling. I would have had to include everything. Instead I had to opt for the truth, for a kind of freedom in the telling, for a kind of selective vision that was mine only, had to leave out and shore up, simplify and shine up. I could not have had a better introduction to the Muse if I had shaken hands.

And so I wrote, and with the freedom of this new writing went on to a companion sestina about my grandfather, whom I had never met, and another about great-aunts. There was no stopping me now that I had found this new angle on truth. I had in fact found the way once again. And it *was*, after all, easy; it's just that it was hard.

I chose the sestina form because it was hard, and I'd just learned about it, and this seemed the thing to match the new small epiphany I was going through. Well, and also, it was an assignment. The truth of the whole thing is that the best parts of the story—the realizations about the poem's importance, and all the rest—came well after the poem. But the poem carried those things in it, had a kind of prescience. A good thing to discover; it keeps one from having to invent things about the work.

I think too that the sestina came as a kind of car to me. I became a writer because I could do it, if I may simplify. My brother could fix cars, my father could do everything, my mother could be a nurse and cook. They all came home greasy in their various ways. I had to find something, and took comfort in the kind of car a sestina was, could work at fixing its engine, polishing its fins, calling it a Dodge.

Sestina later began to mean simply working at a poem. But it was nice to call work something else, and to enjoy it. To find I had been doing it all along. To call it poetry. And I could find, though I tried, no other job where I could use those snags and bits, those things—"the cereal smell of urine"—that kept haunting me.

The Paterson Public Library

It was a Greek temple in the ruins of an American city. To get to it I had to walk through neighborhoods where not even the carcasses of rusted cars on blocks or the death traps of discarded appliances were parted with, so that the yards of the borderline poor, people who lived not in a huge building, as I did, but in their own decrepit little houses, looked like a reversed archeological site, incongruous next to the pillared palace of the Paterson Public library.

The library must have been built during Paterson, New Jersey's, boom years as the model industrial city of the North. Enough marble was used in its construction to have kept several Michelangelos busily satisfied for a lifetime. Two roaring lions, taller than a grammar school girl, greeted those brave enough to seek answers there. Another memorable detail about the façade of this most important place to me were the phrases carved deeply into the walls—perhaps the immortal words of Greek philosophers—I could not tell since I was developing astigmatism at that time and could only make out the lovely geometric designs they made.

All during the school week I both anticipated and feared the long walk to the library because it took me through enemy territory. The black girl Lorraine, who had chosen me to hate and terrorize with threats at school, lived in one of the gloomy little houses that circled the library like sackclothed suppliants. Lorraine would eventually carry out her violence against me by beating me up in a confrontation formally announced through the school grapevine so that for days I lived with a panic that has rarely been equaled in my adult life, since now I can get grown-ups to listen to me, and at that time disasters had to be a fait accompli for a teacher or a parent to get involved. Why did Lorraine hate me? For reasons neither one of us fully understood at the time. All I remember was that our sixth-grade teacher seemed to favor me, and her way of showing it was by having me tutor "slow" students in spelling and grammar. Lorraine, older and bigger than myself since she was repeating the grade, was subjected to this ritual humiliation, which involved sitting in the hallway, obviously separated from the class—one of us for being smart, the other for the opposite reason. Lorraine resisted my efforts to teach her the basic rules of spelling. She would hiss her threats at me, addressing me as *"You little Spic."* Her hostility sent shudders through me. But baffling as it was, I also accepted it as inevitable. She would beat me up. I told my mother and the teacher, and they both reassured me in vague adult terms that a girl like Lorraine would not dare get in trouble again. She had a history of problems that made her a likely candidate for reform school. But Lorraine and I knew that the violence she harbored had found a target: me—the skinny Puerto Rican girl whose father was away with the navy most of the time and whose mother did not speak English; I was the perfect choice.

Thoughts like these occupied my mind as I walked to the library on Saturday mornings. But my need for books was strong enough to propel me down the dreary streets with their slush-covered sidewalks and the skinny trees of winter looking like dark figures from a distance: angry black girls waiting to attack me.

But the sight of the building was enough to reassure me that sanctuary was within reach. Inside the glass doors was the inexhaustible treasure of books, and I made my way through the stacks like the beggar invited to the wedding feast. I remember the musty, organic smell of the library, so different from the air outside. It was the smell of an ancient forest, and since the first books that I read for pleasure were fairy tales, the aroma of transforming wood suited me as a prop.

With my pink library card I was allowed to check out two books from the first floor—the children's section. I would take the full hour my mother had given me (generously adding fifteen minutes to get home before she sent my brother after me) to choose the books I would take home for the week. I made my way first through the world's fairy tales. Here I discovered that there is a Cinderella in every culture, that she didn't necessarily have the white skin and rosy cheeks Walt Disney had given her, and that the prince they all waited for could appear in any color, shape, or form. The prince didn't even have to be a man.

It was the way I absorbed fantasy in those days that gave me the sense of inner freedom, a feeling of power and the ability to fly that is the main reward of the writer. As I read those stories I became not only the characters but their creator. I am still fascinated by the idea that fairy tales and fables are part of humankind's collective unconscious—a familiar theory that acquires concreteness in my own writing today, when I discover over and over that the character I create or the themes that recur in my poems and in my fiction are my own versions of the "types" I learned to recognize very early in my life in fairy tales.

There was also violence in these stories: villains decapitated in honorable battle, goblins and witches pursued, beaten, and burned at the stake by heroes with magic weapons possessing the supernatural strength granted to the self-righteous in folklore. I understood those black-and-white duels between evil and justice. But Lorraine's blind hatred of my person and my knee-liquifying fear of her were not so clear to me at that time. It would be many years before I learned about the politics of race, before I internalized the awful reality of the struggle for territory that underscored the lives of blacks and Puerto

Ricans in Paterson during my childhood. Each job given to a light-skinned Hispanic was one less job for a black man; every apartment leased to a Puerto Rican family was one less place available to them. Worst of all, though the Puerto Rican children had to master a new language in the schools and were often subjected to the scorn and impatience of teachers burdened with too many students making too many demands in a classroom, the blacks were obviously the ones singled out for "special" treatment. In other words, whenever possible they were assigned to special education classes in order to relieve the teacher's workload, mainly because their black English dialect sounded "ungrammatical" and "illiterate" to our white Seton Hall University and City College–educated instructors. I have on occasion become angry at being treated like I'm mentally deficient by persons who make that prejudgment upon hearing an unfamiliar accent. I can only imagine what it must have been like for children like Lorraine, whose skin color alone put her in a pigeonhole she felt she had to fight her way out of every day of her life.

I was one of the lucky ones; as an insatiable reader I quickly became more than adept at the use of the English language. My life as a navy brat, moving with my family from Paterson to Puerto Rico every few months as my father's tours of duty demanded, taught me to depend on knowledge as my main source of security. What I learned from books borrowed from the Greek temple among the ruins of the city, I carried with me as the lightest of carry-on luggage. My teachers in both countries treated me well in general. The easiest way to become a teacher's pet, or *la favorita*, is to ask the teacher for books to read—and I was always looking for reading material, even my mother's romantic novels by Corin Tellado and her *Buenhogar* (Spanish *Good Housekeeping* magazine) were not safe from my insatiable word hunger.

Since the days when I was stalked by Lorraine, libraries have always been an adventure for me. Fear of an ambush is no longer the reason why I feel my pulse quicken a little when I approach a library building, when I enter the stacks and inhale the familiar smell of old leather and paper. It may be the memory of the danger that heightens my senses, but it is really the expectation that I felt then and that I still feel now about books. I gained confidence in my intelligence by reading books. They contained most of the information I needed to survive in two languages and in two worlds. When adults were too busy to answer my endless questions, I could always look it up; when I felt unbearably lonely, as I often did during those early gypsy years traveling with my family, I read to escape, and also to connect: you can come back to a book as you cannot always to a person or place you miss. I read and reread favorite books until the characters seemed like relatives or friends I could see when I wanted or needed to see them.

I still feel that way about books. They represent my spiritual life. A library is my sanctuary, and I am always at home in one. It is not surprising that in recalling my first library, the Paterson Public Library, I have always described it as a temple.

Lorraine carried out her threat. One day after school, as several of our classmates, Puerto Rican and black, circled us to watch, Lorraine grabbed a handful of my long hair and forced me to my knees. Then she slapped my face hard enough that the sound echoed off the brick walls of the school building and ran off while I screamed at the sight of blood on my white knee socks and felt the throbbing on my scalp where I would have a bald spot advertising my shame for weeks to come.

No one intervened. To this crowd, it was one of many such violent scenes taking place among the adults and the children of people fighting over a rapidly shrinking territory. It happens in the jungle and it happens in the city. But another course of action other than "fight or flight" is open to those of us lucky enough to discover it and that is channeling one's anger and energy into the development of a mental life. It requires something like obsessiveness for a young person growing up in an environment where physical labor and physical endurance are the marks of a survivor—as is the case with minority peoples living in large cities. But many of us do manage to discover books. In my case, it may have been what anthropologists call a cultural adaptation. Being physically small, non–English speaking, and always the new kid on the block, I was forced to look for an alternate mode to survival in Paterson. Reading books empowered me.

Even now, a visit to the library recharges the batteries in my brain. Looking through the card catalog reassures me that there is no subject I cannot investigate, no world I cannot explore. Everything that is, is mine for the asking. Because I can read about it.

At an Artists Colony

Black Arms

A group of us are sitting around the TV room. Ray, a painter from the South, is talking about how hard his mother works. He says: "I told her all you need is a pair of good black arms." The others snicker.

I am new here. All I want to do is get along. I say nothing, though now I know there is a part of me that is a joke to this man—my washerwoman great-grandmother, my cook grandmother.

I will be silent. I want him to like me. I want to tell him how he hurts me. I want to speak. But then the colonists will say, "You know how sensitive they are." I will be labeled. And for six weeks, the only black person, I will never be able to sit at the dinner table without "Black Arms."

Dinner Time

Last night at the dinner table, John, a man who didn't know I'm black, noticed the book of women's diary writing which has a section of *The Black Notebooks* in it.

He asked me to see the book, and when he took it I could see he wasn't going to just skim over the table of contents. He went directly for my story, putting down his fork, and began to read. I felt a coldness, like a breeze ruffling a curtain on the line. The other dinner tables were quiet; many of the colonists don't know I'm black. I could just hear him blurt loudly, "I didn't know you're black. You don't look black. How did you get that color?"

I don't like to lose control of my identity that way. I fear being the center of attention, like an animal in a cage prodded and poked by onlookers.

The man, fortunately, kept his comments to the quality of the work. "This is great. It sent a shiver up my spine. It's dramatic."

The other people at the table didn't know the content. Not that I mind every person at the colony knowing I'm black. I don't care, and I am proud of my work. But when several come at me from all sides, I don't know which way to turn. Heaven help me if I should show anger or be defensive.

John wouldn't let it alone. Later, as several of us were sitting around the fireplace, he said, "You should read this article in the *Times*. You'll like it. It reminds me of your book." I hadn't seen the article, but I knew it must be about black people. As soon as he knew I am black, I became a category, and now anything he reads by or about a black person reminds him of me.

A Chinese man who has also read my book said, "This article is nothing like the writing in Toi's book." I was glad he spoke, defending the uniqueness of my experience.

Later, John was playing pool. I was sitting twenty feet away and noticed him staring at me. I thought he was thinking I was attractive and was beginning to feel flattered. Suddenly he yelled across the room, "You really should read that article. You'll find it interesting. It's really timely."

Another man in the room called: "What's the article about?"

"Racism," he yelled back.

The people in the room looked up. I felt the conversation go out of my hands.

The other man said, "That isn't timely. It's ongoing and eternal."

I was glad somebody spoke and it wasn't me.

The Testimony of Innocence

Last night I went over to Marty's studio to share my work. She read some of my diary entries and I read some of her poems. She said she felt my diary entries were extremely important. She asked me whom they were addressed to, and I read her the entry that describes my audience: all the people in my past, black and white, who represent the internalized process of racism within me.

In 1976, when I began writing *The Black Notebooks*, I wrote mainly to myself, although at the back of my mind was an idea that maybe someday I would find the courage to make it public. The idea was to tell the truth as deeply as I could, however painful, but also to write for a larger human community. I know that sounds ridiculously grandiose, but I felt an honest confession would have merit. My negative self-concept made me trust myself to be more egoless than some writers whose descriptions of racism seem to be testimonies of their own innocence—and I have always distrusted that, from both whites and blacks.

My skin color causes certain problems continuously, problems that open the issue of racism over and over, like a wound, a chronic wound—a stigmata. These openings are occasions for reexamination. My skin color keeps things, literally, from being either black or white.

My decision to make more of my entries public comes from my meeting at the colony with a political activist, Pat, who, when I showed her the entries which are most shameful to me, entries which show my repulsion for other blacks, still loved me, showed me the mirror of acceptance. How I love her for that!

I'll publish. I'll make a name for myself; I'll make money. I'll win the love of my relatives and get a full professorship at a university. I'll win a movie contract and play the heroine of my own story. It seems awful to hope success will come out of such disaster.

Not to worry, Pat says, writing about racism doesn't make you successful, it makes you ignored.

Ray

Yesterday, after breakfast, I saw him lumbering toward his jeep. He looked a little lost; several of his close friends have left the colony. I had heard him say another gem this morning, "I wish I had ten little black women to sew the holes in that canvas . . ."

Every time the opportunity comes to talk to him the time doesn't seem right. Either other people are around or there's another problem. After his art show last night, I stayed longer than anyone, but he seemed depressed with people's reactions. It would have been piling shit on top of shit if I had tried to talk to him; and I don't think he would have heard what I was saying. I found myself listening to his worries, reassuring him, and kicking myself for being a coward.

But this morning was perfect. I know he often goes into town for donuts. I had been on my way to my studio, but I turned in my tracks.

Sitting in the donut shop, I waited for a relaxed moment. The comforting cups of coffee were placed before us. He lit a cigarette. "There's something I have to tell you," I said. "I'm black, and last week when you made that comment about black arms, it made me feel bad. And this morning you said something else about little black women sewing holes in the canvas." I didn't say it in a mean voice, just a human voice, one on one. (Inside, I'm saying, Why can't I just blurt it out? Why do I have to be so careful?)

I tried not to look at his face so I could get my words out, but I caught a glimpse and saw a muscle twitching in his cheek; his mouth was slightly open, and he was listening to me intently. I went on, "You see, I wanted to say something to you when this happened last week, but I didn't want to say something that would make people look at me as if I'm different. Sometimes when people find out I'm black, they treat me differently from then on. So when people say things that hurt me, I don't know what to do. I want to tell them. But, at the same time, I'm afraid I'll be hurt even more if I do."

He started to explain. "When I said that about 'black arms,' I was repeating something my mother-in-law said, and I was repeating it because I was horrified by it. What you feel must be similar to what I feel at my wife's house, because I am the only goy." I was happy that he was identifying with me, but I hate it when, after I let a white person know they've said something racist, I end up having to listen for hours to the story of their life. I just wanted to tell him my pain and make sure he got my message. "Please, I don't want to put you on the spot. I just want you to understand my feelings. Do you understand? What do you hear me saying?" He said, "I hear you saying that certain comments which other people make without sensitivity have great poignancy to you because you are black." That wasn't exactly what I was saying, but it seemed close. Besides, it had taken all the bravery I could muster to come this far, I couldn't press him further.

In the past, I have left conversations like this empty, not getting what I wanted. I thought it was rage I wanted to vent. But yesterday, because he listened, because I had waited for the right moment and asked for what I wanted, I thought, maybe I've found the answer. From now on, if I just wait, if I just talk about my feelings honestly, if I don't expect the person to say something to take my pain away, if I just ask him or her to repeat back what I said until they've understood, then everything will be fine.

I want so much to find a formula! Of course, there is none. Sometimes it will come out OK, like yesterday, and sometimes I will walk away with a hole in my heart that all the little black women in the world cannot sew up.

Saturday Night

Several colonists sat around trying to have fun on a Saturday night. We miss New York, movies, Chinese restaurants. We talked about feminism, about how, these days, many of the young girls have babies while in high school.

A southern lady said, "That's what black girls have been doing for years. They have babies and their families raise them. Maybe it's catching up with white girls." This is the same woman who three days ago was talking about how black people have "funny" names. "They name their kids the strangest things." I thought about the twins in New Jersey whose mother had honored the doctor who had delivered them by giving them names he suggested: Syphily and Gonorra.

This woman loves to talk about black people. She's our resident expert. She said, "There aren't any black people here. I haven't seen any."

"Yes there are," I said, smiling.

"Who?"

"You're looking at one."

"You're not really black. Just an eighth or something."

"I don't know how black I am, but I am black."

"Was your mother black?"

"My mother, my father, my grandparents. They are black, and they look just like me."

"How do you know you're black?"

"I'm black because black people were the first people I touched and loved."

A woman at the table said, "Did you read the article in the *New York Times* that said if they were strict about genetics, sixty percent of the people in the United States would be classified as black?"

I looked around the table. I was laughing. The others were not. They were worried about how black I was, and they should have been worrying about how black *they* are.

I thought of all the little white children, the light of their mothers' and fathers' eyes, in Montana, in flat Wyoming, in Idaho, in lakey Michigan; I thought of that "funny" blackness inside of them, a kernel in each little heart put there, somehow in the night, like a visit from the tooth fairy.

I thought of the layers of lies of the first generation that covered that mystery up, the layers of repressed questions in the second generation which decomposed into layers of unconsciousness. Layer after layer, till one day children walk around with unconsciousness laid over their minds like shrouds, pretty little children in pinafores with a nigger maid who has a funny name. Somewhere babies are popping out of women and no one understands where they come from.

I smile at the heart of darkness in sixty out of a hundred babies. The drop of blood that can't lie to statistics, that will be bled out, measured, and put in a crystal tube.

That blood gives those little ones a special light. Wherever I look I see brothers, sisters, who want to break out of their cramped skins, singing with love.

That

Marty said yesterday she was surprised that Pat had called the colony a "white establishment" and said she was uncomfortable with some of the people. Marty hadn't noticed any of "that." Had I noticed any of "that"?

I was on guard. So many times, if a black person admits discomfort, the white person then says that the black person must be "sensitive"—paranoid—responding not to the present environment, which is safe and friendly, but to something in the past. They want to hear that the white people in this environment (themselves) are fine. It's the black person who is crazy.

I said, "It is not something that is done consciously; but most of the white people here have had limited exposure to blacks; there are bound to be great problems in communication. There are some people who hate and fear blacks and don't want to be under the same roof. For example, Jan told me what Sandra said when she saw no black people in the dining room: "Good. I'm glad there are no black people. After New York, this is refreshing."

Marty said sometimes when she is with black people, she doesn't know what to do; no matter what she does it seems to be the wrong thing.

She told me how she had invited a black woman, a lawyer, over to her house for dinner, and during the dinner conversation the guests at the table started talking about Arabs raising the price of everything in England. Marty said she didn't think they were saying anything racist, and even if they were, what did the Arabs have to do with this black woman? But the woman stood up from the table and said, "I'm sorry, I find this conversation extremely embarrassing." Marty asked me did I think the woman was right to do that?

I told her, "Marty, frequently white people who have been made uncomfortable by something a black person says or does go to another black person to try to ease the pain, to feel vindicated. First of all, I wasn't there, so I don't know what she responded to. Secondly, there would be no way to find out unless both of you could sit down and really talk to each other."

Marty said, "That will never happen because she has never asked me out, and when I called her she was cold."

I said, "Black people don't like pain either."

I thought of how sad it is—how a black person and a white person are not just two individuals who have to decide whether they like each other, but representatives carrying huge expectations, stereotypes they must scale like dangerous mountains trying to reach each other.

Jan's Studio

I visited Jan yesterday. I went there feeling greatly honored that she had asked me, since most artists prize their time alone and don't want to be disturbed. I had just come into her room, sat down on the mattress, and received a cup of tea when she took off Mozart and asked if I wanted to hear one of her favorite records, a record about Attica. The hair on the back of my neck stood up. What connection had she made between me and Attica?

Give her a chance, I thought, calming myself, maybe it's just a coincidence.

It was atrocious. A white band had taken the words of a prisoner as he was leaving prison and repeated them over and over as if we were certain to catch the significance. Atonal music played in the background; everything got louder and crashed to an end.

I sat there feeling the need to receive her gift with enthusiasm. She waited. The only word that came to my mind was "interesting."

After she took the record off, she started flipping through her collection of classical music to find something else especially for me. "I have a record by Paul Robeson. Would you like to hear that?" Oh God, I thought, it wasn't a coincidence.

"No, thank you."

She seemed puzzled and at a loss. Finally, she asked, "There is a picture around here of a black man I liked. I slept with him. Would you like to see that?"

I gaped at her innocent face: Jan, the woman I head toward at dinner time because she is not pompous or intimidating, one of the only people here I feel comfortable with.

I told her that just because I am black doesn't mean I am one dimensional. I am interested in many things, just as she is. I like classical music and know quite a bit about it. She said, "But my other black friends like it when I play those records." She looked genuinely hurt.

I told her all black people are different. She said, "But I've tried so hard. I'm tired of always trying to please them." She looked at me in anger. I was one more proof of her inadequacy as if I should have taken whatever was offered and let her feel generous and good.

I left abruptly, sorry for my anger, sorry for what I had learned about her, sorry that she had lost her feeling of closeness, however illusory, to black people—sorry, sorry, sorry—and somehow to blame. I had felt close to her, now I distrusted my instincts and dreaded a deeper isolation here than ever before.

Jazz

Now that I am the "known" black here, everything with a tinge of blackness on it is delivered to me.

Mark, the composer, who has been talking about Mozart at

the dinner table for days, comes running up to me this afternoon when he sees me on the path, his face lit like a beacon. He doesn't even bother with a greeting.

"Guess what I've been doing today?" he blurts out.

I can't imagine.

"I've been writing JAZZ," he presents, as if it is a Cartier jewel on a silver platter.

What am I supposed to say? You must be a really nice white guy? Thanks for taking us seriously?

"Good for you," I answer, and walk on as quickly as possible.

Crazy Thoughts

How beautiful the view from my desk of wildflowers through the cathedral-tall window. I watch the lovely black birds. How kind the lunch on my doorstep, the vegetable torte with white cream sauce, the chocolate cake. How pleasing the flower on the table, the yellow Victorian sofa, the barn of colorful chickens. Kind and specific the words in the office, the locks on my doors. I am treated like a queen. But when the lights go off, I face my fears.

Why is my stomach in knots? Why do I fear that during the night I'll be smothered? I think poison gas will come out of the register. I think the people are monsters, not artists, and during the night they will implant a small radio in my brain. How can I think this? Memory of my father being smothered by a pillow my grandmother put over his head when he was three? In the morning I am ashamed.

I try desperately to make friends, hoping I will actually feel that trust that makes the knots in my stomach loosen. I was terrified to come here; I always feel frightened, except when I'm near home. I trust no one—especially not myself.

I try to do my work. This is a perfect environment. No cleaning. No cooking. I needn't even go to get my lunch; it is placed in a basket outside my door by a man on tiptoes. Wood is stacked. I make a fire. I sit in the sun. I want to be grateful. I am grateful. But the sickness of fear backs up in my throat like phlegm.

In the kitchen the cook speaks softly. I want to sit by her all day and stay away from the roads on which I have been hurt by a word. But she is cooking and I don't want to bother her.

Please, let me not bother anyone or anything. Let me leave the tub without a hair. Let me not speak to those who turn their bodies slightly away from me. I must notice this.

No one can help. Only I, myself. But how can I let go? My face is a mask, like Uncle Tom's, my heart twisted in rage and fear.

After

After I came back I was sick for several weeks. I felt completely wrung out, run-down. I had left smiling, beaming, thanking everyone—the kitchen help, the office help, the yard help—for their kindness. My friend came to pick me up. The night before we were to drive home, I sat with her in the restaurant— the first black face I had seen in weeks—and, for an instant, I felt my body falling under me, as if I had slipped under the wheels of a train. I had made it until the last minute, keeping a stiff upper lip, and here I was, so close to the end, finally about to lose it.

They were so sorry to see me go that they offered me a stay of two more weeks. If I stayed I would prove my desperate bravery to myself. But I declined. I was tired of feeling frightened and wanted to go home where I felt safe.

A Jewish activist friend returned from the colony shortly after and asked me to please write a letter telling how hard it was to be the only black person there. She had found the same token black during her stay. I postponed it and postponed it. I didn't want to do it. I had been a success—I had gone some-place far from home and stayed four weeks without having a nervous breakdown. And they had tried to do everything to please me—cook, clean up after me, put wood in my fireplace. I didn't have the heart to tell them I had been miserable and frightened all the time. Besides, I wanted to be a "success-ful" black person, a person they would ask back, a person who would ease the way for other blacks. "See, we're not as bad as you thought."

The day my friend returned from the colony she was full of news about how she had written a letter to the board, sent names and addresses of black artists. The president had talked to her for a half hour about how pleased he was with her efforts. The next day she called me, despondent. Her editor had called her from her large publishing house—they were remainder-ing her last book. I felt so sorry for her. I told my husband about her efforts at the colony and how she had come home to this big disappointment. "I'm not surprised," he said. "Somebody from the colony must have gotten to somebody at her publish-ing house and iced her." I looked at my husband angrily. "Oh, that's silly," I said. "One has nothing to do with the other." But I felt the ground under me sinking.

Black Catholics:
Cultural Exiles, Literary Exiles

from "Evangeline"

years slide away   two four five
and the loneliness gradually simply annoys
like a rollerskate scar on your knee
when you are all dressed up or at the beach
loneliness on the girls' side of the church
because your mother and your brothers never change
never dare to risk what you must
confess and confess every week
loneliness among the girls next door
down the block around the corner
you like them bald-
head nuns?   *why they priest dont marry them?*
dont they sweat in the summer?   *can they wear*
bathing suits?   *you aint never seen no colored*
nuns, right?   *they aint got no colored, right?*
loneliness in the words you know how to defend:
indulgence Extreme Unction catechumens
words you may never use
Immaculate Conception Trinity purgatory
at the family Thanksgiving Christmas Easter
mornings when all your kinship parades itself
against the dark stubborn defeated souls
rejoice not one of us out-of-doors
not one of us in jail crippled blind ragboned

in this politely unbrotherly city
alleluia
loneliness in your exemptions from school:
Ascension Thursday All Saints' Day St. Patrick
loneliness in your holy water
your rosary miraculous medal scapular holy cards . . .
then on your sixth first day of school
a boy steps through the invisible door
a family of boys colored and African-looking
like the martyrs of Uganda
you've never seen but imagine really dark
and you rejoice you share the mark though
you barely say hello
as your history moans
you share the mark

In May 1990 I attended a day-long symposium on African-American Religion: Problems and Resources for the 1990s. Held at Harlem, New York's, Schomburg Center for Research in Black Culture, the four panels concentrated on issues of denominational research, local history, church music, and regionalism. The speakers, some of whom were clergy, presented papers dealing exclusively with the Black Protestant religious experience in the United States.

Unlike the African Muslims in the audience, whose questions to the panelists insinuated an underlying annoyance with the Protestant exclusivity of the program, I was neither surprised nor strongly perturbed. A native-born American, I had known long before my own systematic perusal of American history and literature that the term *Black church* meant Protestant. Period. The tradition to which I belong, Roman Catholicism, is not treated by the Black community as if it were an essential part of the Black American religious experience.

For example, in standard Black history texts, little or no

coverage is afforded the community contributions of Catholic educators like the Black nuns of Baltimore during the early years of emancipation. Even the high profile given to the free Blacks of New Orleans during the Civil War is bound most prominently to their mulatto status. Their Catholicism, with its realized or potential link to the Caribbean cultures and politics of that time, is never explored.

Likewise, in contemporary media Black Catholicism is never viewed as a significant culture-making presence in the community. On occasion, such as the visit of Pope John Paul II in the 1980s to the Harlem church, St. Charles Borromeo, Black Catholicism is trotted out of the closet and put on display. Virtually ignored in the media, however, is the positive day-to-day role of Catholic elementary schools, which are low-cost private institutions perceived as alternatives to public miseducation in Black neighborhoods by many non-Catholics to the degree that some convert to Catholicism in order to enroll their children.

On the other hand, discord within Catholic ranks is always given the spotlight in the United States news media, from a national issue like abortion to the censure of a theologian at a Catholic university; hence the recent front-page coverage of the Imani Church, a Black Catholic schism in Washington, D.C.

Certainly Black Catholics are not the only minority within the African-American race that suffers from a "buried identity." Black Native Americans, Blacks from the Midwest and West, and, until recently, Black Caribbeans were assigned "bit parts" and "walk-ons" in the bloody tragedy of New World slavery, emancipation, and delayed empowerment. An oversimplified analysis of the slave trade has prompted United States history scholars to minimize the political and cultural movements in the Caribbean and to focus almost exclusively on "Slavery and Emancipation in the Southern States," "Reconstruction," and "The Great Migration North." Black settlement of the West and Midwest (with its not infrequent interface of African and Native American populations) is a mere footnote in the turbulent saga of progress and setbacks.

Those minorities with limited access to and control of the intricate network of cultural dissemination, namely academia and publishing, suffer the peculiar anxieties of being unnoticed or unrecorded, stereotyped or commercially exploited. This is actually an ancient phenomenon only recently diagnosed, analyzed, and addressed. Minorities within minorities remain an untapped source of psychological and sociological enlightenment. Moreover, the minority designation is a relative matter. Considered a minority in the United States, Blacks may have to be defined otherwise from a global perspective. Likewise, while Black Catholics assume a curiously low profile among English-speaking native-born United States citizens, the Black populations of South America and the Caribbean are overwhelmingly Catholic. (An interesting digression from the New World considerations of this essay is the Coptic Christian church of East Africa, which may boast of being not only one of the oldest Christian churches and the cradle of monasticism, but also one of the Eastern traditions still in union with Rome. The major break between the Western and Eastern Christian traditions occurred in the eleventh century.) Yet, despite this African ancestry, it is the irony of ironies that among the Black masses and intelligentsia, Catholicism is perceived to be a "White" religion. Sadly, some Black Catholics do perceive their religion to be a higher form of worship—more dignified, reserved, elegant, full of pomp and circumstance, superior even to the high-toned Episcopalian church because it is more ancient and has the Roman pope for its earthly leader.

It can be conservatively assumed that significant numbers of English-speaking Black North Americans are ignorant of the full history of the religion they profess (be it Protestantism or Catholicism). It can also be conjectured that through the increased migration of Catholic Hispanics into the United States,

Blacks and other Americans are due for a little reeducation. Hispanic Catholicism is a complex mélange of three great cultural traditions: African, Native American, and Spanish/Portuguese. The oversimplified definitions of culture, race, and ethnicity that have operated in the United States will be challenged as never before.

But what does this discussion of Protestantism and Catholicism have to do with American literature? Precisely this: through its major contribution to music and language, the Black Protestant church forms the most fundamental pillar of Black culture in the North American hemisphere. If the struggle for full humanity has been the bone and marrow of the Black American experience, then the Black Protestant culture has been its nourishing, pulsating bloodline. Any Black artist who wishes to write, compose, or perform must acknowledge, uphold, or contend with this Black church tradition. For better or for worse, it cannot be ignored or dismissed. For the non-Protestant Black artist, it is not unlike the relationship all Blacks have with European history and culture.

Whether we have been colonized or enslaved, no matter the degree to which we have adopted Western forms of civilization, each Black must acknowledge and assess the European presence and impact on African peoples everywhere. Unlike the powerful or the hopeless or the complacent, the oppressed who actively resolve to be free must know both sides of the equation thoroughly in order to survive. Blacks may fret and sometimes rebel at the weight of the necessary work to be done and the knowledge to be acquired, for we must know "the Other" as intimately as we know ourselves. This duality of our lives can be extremely debilitating, almost paralyzing. Yet, in a world controlled largely by Western ideologies and institutions, there is no other viable alternative. We hope only to be able to delve into the depths of another cultural perspective without drowning, without losing our own richness, our Black souls.

A similar dilemma confronts the Black artist whose background deviates from the classic North American paradigm: southern origin, enslavement until the Civil War, rural then urbanized through migration north, usually after Reconstruction, pure African descent to highly mixed with European blood, Protestant. This skeletal identity is fleshed in with specifics: a varied region-specific cuisine, a certain way of talking, walking, gesturing, singing, dancing, making music, telling stories, joking. Particular rituals for relations with the opposite sex, particular forms and styles of worship, particular attitudes and preferences in dress and cosmetic design: a worldview. Whether this southern-based Black Protestant aesthetic functions to the same degree throughout the United States, I do not know. But in the community where I grew up, the Philadelphia of the 1950s and 1960s, Blacks assumed a common experience and language upon meeting one another. There was little recognition that one Black could be legitimately different from another in culture. Any difference was viewed as "acting White," being deviant. These deviations could be as serious as bookishness or as trivial as colloquial pronunciation. If unchanged, these deviations could result in total exclusion from social arrangements or relegation to the bottom of the pecking order.

Philosophically, it may be a bit comforting to realize that among themselves Blacks can be as mean-spirited and cliquish as other groups of people. The oppressed are not, by definition, more moral in all matters than the oppressor. I recall with some humor the subtle snipes my Irish Catholic classmates meted out to the handful of Italian and Polish students in that lower-middle-class West Philadelphia parish of my childhood. (Decades later, in Yonkers, this ethnic balance of power was reversed in the small Catholic academy attended by my daughter.) Of course, philosophy is hardly comforting to one who is young and developing an identity to which "tribal" obstacles seem arbitrary and insurmountable. Rejection can be devastating. (I wonder about the course of Jimi Hendrix's life and career had he not been raised in a Catholic environment. To this day, unlike their White contemporaries, Blacks of my generation do not laud Hendrix as an innovative genius of the electric blues guitar.) At times, rejection can transform someone who may have been only curiously different into a cultural pariah.

Those who are different may occasionally feel cheated by fate. Decisions made by one generation must be paid for by the next. Parents may be significantly responsible for a child's deviancy—it was they who decided to move far away from their place of birth, it was they who decided to marry someone of another race or ethnic group, it was they who decided to change their religion, or to have none at all. Often these decisions have had immediate positive ramifications—political or religious freedom, better economic opportunity, free education. Certainly no normal parent desires his or her offspring to be branded a priori with the scarlet letter *D*. Nevertheless, any choice away from the dominant cultural pattern, if improperly prepared for, can lead to serious drawbacks.

In my own case, my mother's decision to return to Catholicism after a brief experiment with Episcopalianism sealed my fate as a literary deviant. It effectively narrowed my future Black readership and audience. Not only did her decision separate me from an obviously Black American music and language, it also separated me from a Black sociopolitical network (which I shall discuss in more detail presently). Without my assent, a sisterhood, brotherhood, and family were lost to me; an essential camaraderie was forfeited. I was made an exile.

In addition, by enrolling me into all-White Catholic schools in all-White neighborhoods, my mother separated me from other Black Catholics. Mother perceived the other Black parish schools to be inferior to the White ones even though the same orders of nuns taught in both. She did not believe that Whites (even nuns) would teach Black children as thoroughly as they did Whites; surrounded by White children I would receive the same benefits as they. Nor did Mother believe that an all-Black school would prepare me adequately for adult competition with Whites in the job market. There is no doubt in my mind that my mother's assessment of the typical educational environment for northern Blacks in the 1950s—before the civil rights movement, before busing, before affirmative action—was disarmingly correct.

I received an excellent education in Catholic institutions from first grade through college, excelling in all I undertook and becoming a leader among my White peers, all without benefit of special legislation or programs. Nor did I have the personal advantage of college-educated, middle-class parents to "coach" me. With my father's passive consent, my mother threw me into the deep end of the pool and whispered, "Swim." These were the days when "the only Negro" was not quite the maligned cliché among Blacks it has become since the 1970s, along with the other ambivalent sobriquet, "the first Negro."

Yes, in my small, unpublicized West Philadelphia existence, I was "the only" and "the first" quite often, even in a Catholic girls' high school where about fifty other Blacks were in the graduating class. Tracked by first honor grades into courses and sections apart from the others, I became an "untouchable" to them, someone admired, even praised for "making them proud," but always kept at a distance. Even in extracurricular activities where the Black girls tended to segregate themselves voluntarily, I was often the first to cross over the racial boundaries—like the Broadway musicals mounted annually by the Catholic boys' high school. For two years I was the only singer to audition among many fine Black female voices; I was chosen for three shows—bit parts, despite my strong mezzo-soprano range—but wasn't that the tradition? While superstars like Sidney Poitier, Dorothy Dandridge, and Cicely Tyson had given me a standard of professional stamina, these did not seem to inspire the other talented Black girls. (Interestingly, these other girls had attended all-Black parish schools. Again, perhaps my mother's insights had been right on target. Perhaps northern segregated environments did not prepare Blacks psychologically for the most ordinary competitive situations.)

I touch upon my experience as a Catholic student (a matter analyzed further in my essay "A.M.D.G.—Revisited," published in an anthology on competition among women edited by Helen E. Longino and Valerie Miner) because it is generic to all experiences defined as atypical in the Black community. To do something outside the dominant cultural group, to venture out before others follow—even if the result is positive and ultimately beneficial for the group—is neither encouraged nor rewarded enthusiastically. Even when a new perspective on an old truth is heralded, Blacks tend to stand back silently until others give their approval. (The literary career of Alice Walker, a Protestant daughter of the South, is a case in point; not until she had become the premier Black spokeswoman of the contemporary feminist movement with its predominantly White middle-class leadership did she begin to receive adequate and positive attention among Black literary tastemakers.) So, necessary initial recognition is allowed to come from non-Black admirers, but too much recognition from such quarters may be viewed with suspicion and even resentment—Jimi Hendrix is, again, a classic example. This is an ancient story . . . the prophet ignored, ostracized in his own country.

Of course, being a Catholic is hardly identical with genius, let alone prophetic destiny. Nor is Catholicism essentially more beneficial than Protestantism. At its simplest, Catholicism is a mere difference in the performance of worship from the Black North American mainstream. At its most complex, it can be a vicarious, intimate encounter with the evolution of the European mind and soul. Why should a Black want that? Why should one want to stand on the moon? Why should one want to find a defense against AIDS? Etc., etc., etc.

Cultural deviants often function as scouts—again, unasked by the dominant group. Sadly, one's insights into an alien environment may be tardily acknowledged by the "folks back home." Often during the "sojourn in Egypt" one learns patterns of thought incomprehensible and unacceptable to one's own brothers and sisters. As one becomes intimate with Pharoah, one may be perceived, rightly or wrongly, as "selling out." Perhaps the biblical stories reveal a cogent lesson: neither Joseph nor Moses sold out. Rather, the skills they acquired were invaluable to the ultimate survival of their kinspeople.

Similarly do I interpret the cultural potential of Black Catholics in North America. Through a religious tradition and corresponding intellectual discipline, Black Catholics are related to two immense cultural groups that will increasingly affect United States and global events: Hispanic Americans and Eastern Europeans—both, significantly if not predominantly, Catholic. Contrary to United States pop mythology, the average Catholic education is not narrow and medieval. In my so-called rotelike, all-female high school of the early 1960s, I learned more about the foundation of Eastern European culture and politics than my daughter learned in her progressive, science-oriented, co-ed high school in the late 1980s. (Another digression: all Catholic American children of the cold war era prayed for the release of the three "captive" nations of Latvia, Estonia, and Lithuania. I myself was quite familiar with the situation because my best friend in the fifth grade was Lithuanian.) Although South American history did not enjoy then the spotlight it is beginning to attract now, Catholic students back then were vaguely aware of a kinship with Latinos beyond the mere hemispheric or politically ideological.

Whether practicing, lapsed, or actively opposed, of whatever race or ethnicity, a Catholic can use this global religious legacy as a means of primary, even primal, dialogue in a world in which freedom of communication is the least violent defense against all kinds of oppression and repression. A Catholic can use this heritage not simply as an answer or a point of termination but as a starting point, a question. Questions? Within the Catholic church? Indeed, in the educational institutions I attended the required study of Catholic church history (with its considerable lapses from the high road of Christ's exemplary life) was taught developmentally. My introduction to biblical exegesis as a college freshman and sophomore was a far cry from my catechism lessons of first and second grade. Collegiates in Catholic institutions of higher learning did study the major nineteenth- and twentieth-century questions posed by scholarly believers and doubters of Christianity; in particular, what, if any, were the cross-cultural ancient elements that formed the fabric of the seemingly seamless belief we call Catholicism?

An affinity for cross-cultural communication (whether in formalized debate or in personalized persuasion) is the advantage Catholicism can give the Black educated well in that tradition. But as I posit this potential asset, I must also acknowledge a major drawback. A North American Catholic upbringing does not teach Blacks the cultural language necessary to speak with "cousin." Unlike the Black Protestant church, the Catholic experience in North America does not prepare its Black communicants for leadership among Blacks outside Catholicism itself. This is not to say that cultural leaders have not arisen from the ranks of Black Catholicism, but the degree to which a Black has been trained and has excelled in the particular cultural style of North American Catholicism will be the degree of exile he or she will have to transcend.

What is the North American Catholic cultural style and how does it differ from the Black American Protestant style? Composed as it is of many ethnic groups which are culturally varied, if not opposed, the North American Catholic church can be viewed as a single cultural style only when the heart of the religion is described: the Roman Catholic Mass. In pre-Vatican II days, the ordinary Low Mass (spoken, not sung) was characterized by a passive, possibly meditative congregation, which witnessed the reenactment of the ministry, death, and resurrection of the Son of God, Jesus Christ, the Savior of Humanity. In this dramatic homage to the sacrificed god (an ancient global rite documented by scores of scholarly works, the most quoted of which is Frazer's *The Golden Bough*), all vestiges of ritual cannibalism, nature worship, human sexuality, and fecundity had been washed away by the cool, sonorous Latin script, by the formal gestures and regal costumes of the main visible actor (the priest), and by the awesome set design and props (the cold marble altar, the gold cross and chalice). Down to the smallest details (the white linen, the pristine crystal, the acerbic incense), the overriding stylistic goals were reverential more than cathartic, quiescent more than participatory, transcendental more than imminent (despite the culminating rite—the eating of the Holy Eucharist, which Catholics believe to be the transformed body and blood of Christ).

I venture to say that despite all the changes of Vatican II— the use of the vernacular languages, more hymn singing and praying aloud by the congregation, a modernized liturgy and hymnal, lay participation in the rite of the Holy Eucharist—the predominant style and tone of the North American Mass has not changed radically from the description above. Oh yes, there are groups of men and women all across the United States involved in the development of alternative liturgies. Yet, walk into most Catholic churches in middle-class suburbia and you will hear and see the old ways: mumbled praying and singing, sheepish foot-shuffling to the altar for Holy Communion (the

Eucharist), a somewhat hasty, though respectful, exit. For all its display of resplendent accoutrements, for all its long history of congregationally recognized and accepted ritual, the North American Mass remains a somewhat private experience when compared with that of an Abyssinian Baptist or Pentecostal Holiness church.

Again, what does all the above have to do with American literature? Quite simply, all of the above is far from the typical religious experience of Black North Americans. Furthermore, the typical religion of Black North Americans, Protestantism, has played a dominant role in American aesthetics, Black and White and any color in between. Except for Episcopalianism (whose rite is similar to Roman Catholicism, so much so that I walked into the famous Trinity Church on Wall Street in Manhattan several years ago and thought I had stumbled upon a somewhat conservative Catholic church), the Black Protestant religious style is the opposite of North American Catholicism; it is more congregationally participatory, more demonstratively impassioned, more oratorical than ritualistic. A Roman Catholic Mass can be conducted with only the priest present and still be valid ritual; the Black Protestant minister can do nothing (and is nobody) without his congregation. Whereas the Roman Catholic Mass almost seems like a dialogue between the priest and the spiritual, the Black Protestant tradition is a dialogue between minister and congregation. The goal of the Black Protestant service is to "move" a congregation spiritually—and sometimes physically, as in the civil rights movement of the South—through the act of ministerial preaching (and, to no lesser degree, through choir singing). The goal of the Catholic Mass is to "inspire" the congregation through a commemorative and transformative ceremony. These differences are aesthetic as much as they are theological. Each religious tradition has given rise to a great artistic tradition: the West-

ern European theater (including ballet and opera) and Black
American performing arts (from jazz improvisation to an Amiri
Baraka poetry reading).

One might hypothesize that the evolution of the Western
European theatrical tradition has involved a strong movement
away from the intrusion into the art itself by the audience. The
audience is encouraged to be an appreciative witness which
only occasionally makes its presence known through an inter-
mittent "Bravo" (in opera at designated movements) and ap-
plause (usually at the end of a performance). The artistic models are actually structured for this kind of presentation with
clearly demarcated stanzaic patterns in poetry or a set number of acts in drama. In the Western mode the audience is the
passive receiver of the art, as the laity is the private receiver of
the Eucharist. The passivity of the nonartist (the audience or
reader) in the Western tradition reaches its apotheosis in the
rise and dominance of the two quintessential art forms of the
contemporary era: the novel and the cinema. Both art forms
are opposed to the goals of traditional Black art, which is communal and dynamic, full of kinetic simultaneity.

In the United States, where the Black and White artistic traditions have existed side by side, it has been far more difficult
to keep the arts separate than the people who created them.
Is it a coincidence that simultaneous with the surreptitious
interface of Black performers and White audiences through
the modern media of radio and cinema, the twentieth century
has witnessed an accelerated "freeing" of the White audience?
Students of Western drama can testify to various theatrical
movements in the United States and in Europe aimed at tearing down the "fourth wall," that invisible barrier between the
vocal actors on a rectangular proscenium stage and the silent,
receptive audience.

Beyond what can be defined strictly as theater, the Black-
White aesthetic interface has engendered critical ramifications,

not yet adequately analyzed, in modern poetry, certain schools of visual art (including the most recent phenomenon of performance art), video, and contemporary fiction (with the rise of stylistically provocative voices like Toni Morrison and Ishmael Reed). Beyond the purview of this essay is the acknowledged Black ancestry of all successful and abiding American "popular" music arts from the Broadway musical to rock music. Even White gospel singing (via Christian family radio) has become an official category in American cultural history. Apparently, the White artist, regardless of the medium of expression, can borrow from Black artistic traditions freely without the opprobrium of other Whites.

But while Whites imitating Blacks can enjoy financial success and artistic immortality (for example, Allen Ginsberg and the early T. S. Eliot became icons within the jazz-inspired practice of free verse), Black "crossover" artists may expire from the weight of skepticism, neglect, or downright attack. That a Black artist may be as creatively affected by Euro-art forms as a White is by Afro-art is deemed preposterous. In fact, while the term *crossover* is assigned to Black artists who are perceived to use White aesthetics only to attract a White audience, the adverse is rarely true. The White counterpart using Black aesthetic principles is simply being innovative, challenging, or "hip." It is into this puzzling tradition of the so-called crossover that the Black American Catholic artist may be dumped.

Now, *crossover* is a contemporary pop music term, a category designed for marketing, not critical evaluation. Yet, the literary community is not immune to the demands and vagaries of the marketplace. Publication by divisions within the top publishing conglomerates may demand that a writer fit a predetermined slot in the bookstore chains. Even prestigious university presses may defer to prevailing schools or movements in an effort to be culturally correct. But the prevailing schools of thought are created by the most media-visible tastemakers.

These tastemakers are usually concerned with the politically "au courant" (which accounts for their high media profile) as much as they are with the demands of an art form. Who defines the "politically au courant"? Rarely a minority within a minority like Black Catholics, who lack the sociopolitical network of the Black Protestants—which brings me back to the symposium on African-American religion at the Schomburg Center.

Because the foregoing has examined (somewhat cursorily) worship as a performing art with a long-standing influence on the verbal arts, it might be assumed that performance is the decisive difference between the religious (and subsequently aesthetic) traditions of Black Catholics and Black Protestants. Such may not be the case.

As I sat listening to the distinguished panelists at the Schomburg Center symposium I was struck by the composition of the audience. Divided evenly between men and women, it was decidedly unsacerdotal. In all likelihood, most of the men were ministers or church scholars, yet their dark suits and conservative ties could have fit as easily into a corporate board of directors meeting. Displaying greater variety in their dress (from Wall Street suits with a touch of kente cloth to colorful Muslim-inspired attire), the women were predominantly scholars or members of "church families." An elite group— yet one with a strong lay ambience. How very different from the particularly clerical elitism that would have dominated a similar assembly on Catholicism. In these days of feminist consciousness, a Catholic audience might have had a healthy female representation, but I would nevertheless conjecture a male (and priestly) majority among the ranks of speakers and listeners. Even the women present would have been strongly characterized by nuns or former nuns, who, although laity, are perceived by Catholics as members of the clergy.

In Catholicism, those who follow a religious calling (priests, brothers, nuns) are quite distinct from the rest of the congregation. While it may be acceptable that theological issues should be decided by the specialists (the priestly hierarchy), their almost exclusive handling of administrative matters affecting the laity may be more debatable. As the ultimate source of revenue for the parish activities, the laity plays a very subordinate role as decision maker. Whether a new school will be built or an extension added to the church, whether funds will be allocated to a particular domestic or foreign mission— such decisions fall under the jurisdiction of the clergy, whose celibacy strictly sets it apart. Perhaps Catholicism does not sit well with many United States citizens because its clergy seem too much like nobility, a ruling class set apart from the ruled. Undoubtedly, religion is a kind of transcendent political metaphor. The organizational structure of a religion, if not its dogma, will or should mirror the society it serves. Catholicism, in its reluctance to develop a strong lay leadership, seems too authoritarian to democratic United States political philosophy.

As I listened to the Schomburg panelists I marveled at how often they alluded to influential women (usually a pastor's wife, mother, or daughter) who had been the most faithful keepers of church records, archival minutiae of immeasurable value to serious Black scholarship. Time after time Black churchwomen were praised by the panelists and "Amened" by the audience; in financial, humanitarian, missionary, even administrative affairs, they were an indefatigable supporting cast. Of course, as musicians (whether organists or singers) they often usurped the minister's starring role. Within the Black Protestant church this sharing of secular power between men and women, between clergy and laity, is akin to the communal dialogue dominant in the performance of worship. Thus, worship reflects an entire method of operation, a way of being among one another. No similarly egalitarian sociopolitical-liturgical network exists in the North American Catholic church (although the aforementioned Imani Church may be an attempt).

There is an old saying: "Once a Catholic, always a Catholic." It is a mixture of admiration and envy, curiosity and objectivity, that I have brought to all encounters with the Black Protestant church, whether directly (through visits as a child to my maternal great-grandmother's Baptist church) or indirectly (through most major artistic creations by Black North Americans). Intellectually and theologically, I cannot wholeheartedly embrace Protestantism, yet because of its predominance in my own family and race, I am not so much a hostile foreigner in its midst as a circumspect exile. An exile at times from dogma, at times from a particular aesthetics which is an attitude toward art that ultimately embraces an attitude toward community and life itself. Finally, I conjecture "a way home" for me and other Black Catholics involved with the making of art. That roundabout way home is through my affinity for non–North American aesthetics, through more syncretic cultures in which the link between ancient rituals and modern sensibility is subliminally intact, if not actively forged.

War Doll Hotel

When we're young, we record things very fast. Life develops the film. Ritual for sleepless nights: shuffle mental snapshots, fan them out like playing cards. Choose one.

Here's a picture of my mother as a child, rollicking in mud of taro patches, her full-blooded Hawaiian mother, dark, stately, beckoning to her. Here's my mother as a teenager, chasing a mongoose across lava shelves. She's tea-colored and beautiful—broad cheeks, full lips, hair dark, electric. Here's a picture of my father, blonde and pale, a boy in Alabama.

Here's a snapshot that has always troubled me. My father's father, in Decatur, Alabama, in 1921. He's wearing a white robe and a funny cone-shaped hood. Behind him are other men in robes and hoods, and masks with eyeholes. Peekaboo. They're poised, ready for something. You can almost smell the kerosene, hear the crackling wood, the flaming cross. I was twelve when I found that snapshot. Old enough to know. The night I found it, I was afraid to lie down. I fell asleep on my feet like a horse, leaning against the bed I'd barricaded against my door.

This snapshot, too, has troubled me. A picture of Emperor Hirohito and his wife, walking their palace grounds, their dog beside them, leaping and yapping in the sun. It was taken two days before America bombed Hiroshima. I've never understood that dog. Didn't he know what was coming? Aren't animals intuitive? Each time I see that photo in old magazines, that leaping, yapping dog, I think of my father after World War II, taking his Hawaiian wife home to meet his folks in Alabama.

I used to imagine him at the front door of his father's house, puffing his chest out, grinning and proud. He puts his arm around my mother, rings the bell. (Didn't he know what was coming?) They're all assembled inside. Maybe there's a cake, candles lit. WELCOME HOME. Maybe someone sits at a piano, fingers poised above the keys. A window curtain twitches. My father rings and rings but no one ever answers. Finally, he and my mother leave.

This was the late 1940s, a full decade before Hawai'i became a state. A lot of Americans still weren't sure exactly what Hawaiians were. Maybe my father's people thought they were like Nebraskans or Canadians, white folks from far away. Until someone inside the house looked out. What I want to evoke here is not my father's shame, not my mother's humiliation. Not even the silence after he rang the bell. What must be evoked is the twitching of that curtain.

My parents never went south again. They began a life of improvisation and drift. I wonder about my mother in those years, the pain of trying to fit in, her differentness from white, mainland Americans. My father said people saw her as "exotic," which is what one says about those they tend to stare at. By the time I was born they were living back in Honolulu.

Here's a snapshot of my mother running into the sea. I'm six or seven, watching her arms spin gracefully in their sockets, pulling the ocean behind her. She moves like liquid immersed in liquid, and I swim hard to catch up. I tell her I'm confused. I don't know what I am, Hawaiian or Caucasian. *Both*, she says. *What am I first?* I ask. She doesn't hesitate. *Hawaiian.* But I don't look Hawaiian. *You will*, she promises. *It works its way out from the blood.*

Here's a snapshot of me at thirteen, looking down at my mother's grave. In a year my father will desert me, too, going back to Alabama. I don't understand why he leaves me behind. My skin is Anglo pale like his; I have his pale eyes. In other words, I "pass." Years later, I will understand about this man, that the war took his youth and my mother's early death finished him. The rest of his life was epilogue. I would see how that journey south with his dark-skinned bride had been an act of hopeless valor. He must have known what was coming. Maybe marrying her had been an act of courage, too, his passport out of his past. But in the end, played out, he went back to what he knew.

So I grew up in the islands, surrounded by my mother's family, my *'ohana:* dark, handsome, husky men; big, graceful women with a buttery cast to the whites of their eyes. My cousins were all "mix-marriage" offspring: Hawaiian, Chinese, Japanese, Korean, Portuguese, Filipino—dark, tan, yellow, so many hues. I didn't know how happy I was, how secure, locked in the bosom of this large, rollicking, feverish, high-strung clan.

Here's a snapshot of me in summer, working my way through university. I'm standing on the assembly line at Dole packing plant in Honolulu, wearing a steely hairnet, ugly pineapple rash climbing my arms, swearing to myself, *I'm getting out of these nowhere islands. I'm going to the mainland where I belong.* You see the trouble I was in; I still didn't know who I was. I would lose a whole decade, all of my twenties, before I learned that recognizing who you are isn't the subtext of a life. It's the main point. The week I graduated from university, I boarded a flight for New York City, as far from Honolulu as I could get and still be in the United States.

I arrived in the middle of a snowstorm, stepped out of a cab in Manhattan, and started walking toward the brightest lights, which turned out to be the Waldorf-Astoria Hotel. I got as far as the doorman, peered into the lobby of that costly place, and saw what a discrepancy I was. Incongruously, half a block from the Waldorf was the YWCA. I lived there a year, in a room so small I moved around by stealth, by squeezing sideways past the bed. After the shock of those first few days I was swept up in a blizzard of colors, odors, textures of young women flinging themselves through the door of the Y like splendid rag dolls, like glamorous refugees.

They came from everywhere, high-caste women with Ph.D.'s and women whose parents were Gypsies, dragging in their bundles and bags, wearing galoshes and parkas and Chester-fields over shawls, saris, kimonos, and Rasta braids. They came bringing the perfumes of the Orient and the Caribbean and the veldt. Golden East Indians, pale Finns, twins from Kowloon, a Haitian singer, Cubans, South Africans, an Estonian audi-tioning for the American Ballet Theatre, even a beauty queen from Manila.

We were the "foreign residents," apart from the transient population at the Y, drawn together by multi-tongued gabfests in the showers, the cafeteria, by fights, and thefts, and mid-night wailings that seemed to voice a central ache. And there was something else that slowly emerged: a communal scrub-bing down of identities, eccentricities, as we waited for green cards, a husband, a job, degrees.

This was the early 1970s, when the youth of America was still in the throes of hippiedom—headbands, body paint, ragged velvet, glitter, and tat. Yet each morning at the Y, we ironed each other's hair straight, wedged ourselves into cheap high heels and somber-colored little suits that didn't fit the shape of our bodies, then rushed out into corporate New York, hoping to blend. At night, we collapsed in our tiny rooms resembling in-teriors of gypsy caravans, wherein we wiped away the makeup and dragged off the city clothes, exhausted by a world some of us wouldn't achieve.

In time we learned to dress smart, acquire airs, meeting dates for drinks in the bar of the Waldorf, which the twins from Kow-loon pronounced "War . . . dol." The bartenders started calling us their "war dolls," and the Y became War Doll Hotel, from which we fanned out every morning, aiming ourselves at the city. I think the fact that we could do that, that such profoundly dislocated, homesick young women could buoy each other up, assemble, and take *aim;* well, that was the important thing. New York, the target, was insignificant. Targets change.

Of course, for some of us, the city was only on loan, we would have to give it back. These were the women New York broke with blinding exactitude. The suicide, leaping from her window as an afterthought, hair still lathered with shampoo. The student from Caracas who, one night, long sobs tearing from her throat, ran through the halls, scrubbing the walls with her excrement. Paramedics finally pinned her against a door with a needle and syringe, so for a moment she was frozen in the attitude lightning gives its victims. We never saw her again.

Here's a snapshot of that night, five of us huddled, terrified, in someone's room. Sindiwa wacks wet laundry out of the way and calms us down, talking about her three kids left behind in South Africa. White teeth gleaming against her black cheeks and the dazzling bush of her Afro, she tells us how she's going to be a famous journalist. She's twenty-four, older than any of us. She's lived through childbirth, revolutions, and divorce, and she's full of such tremor and dreams; I want to be her friend forever.

And Meena from New Delhi, golden in her saris, her beauty, her gestures so fine they can't be analyzed. A secretary at the UN, she wants to study law, go back to India, and fight for women's rights, for young brides burned to death over dowry disputes, for women denied birth control. But Meena has no funds. Her family disowned her when she refused to marry the husband they chose.

One evening I found her pacing up and down the hall. "You'll make it in this city," she said. "You look white."

I didn't know how to respond. At the Y with my friends, I tried to hold in my whiteness, but out in the city, I held back my Hawaiian side. "Does it bother you . . . being dark?"

Meena shook her head impatiently. "First, Americans look right through you. When they finally *see* you, they stare because you're foreign. When the novelty wears off, they insult you. You're invisible again."

An aunt finally came and took Meena to New Jersey. Sindiwa moved in with a man she met at an interview, and I moved into an apartment with two women I didn't know—robust, racquet-swinging blondes from Massachusetts who'd advertised for a third roommate. Here's a snapshot of me at dinner, describing to them my family's house "on the ocean in Kahala," the millionaire's enclave above Waikiki. They think my family are Caucasians, rich enough to live out there year-round. I never mention my Hawaiian blood.

In time, my roommates introduced me to men from Brown and Amherst, and very quickly these new friends formed certain assumptions about me which sealed me off from any genuine human contact, because those assumptions were false, and I had engendered them. I was beginning to learn about secrets, the ones we move fast to keep ahead of, the fear that at some point they'll get out in front.

After a year as a receptionist at a public relations firm, I started writing press releases for wigs and hair spray, thinking that was writing. Another year passed. I kept in touch sporadically with Sindiwa and Meena and my family in Honolulu, took writing courses at New York University, sent short stories to magazines, filed the rejection letters, changed jobs, and after several more years married a lawyer, an older man, pale and blonde as my father had been. I sent my father snapshots, needing to show this man who had deserted me that I'd replaced him. He wished me happiness, and just seeing his handwriting triggered a meltdown in my body chemistry, like lovesickness or deathly fear.

Like all marriages, ours dipped and soared. My husband encouraged me in my writing and seemed to take pride in my Hawaiian background, conjuring for his friends my family in Honolulu as "Dutch with a touch of Hawaiian blood." (In fact, it was the other way around.) I became his "island aristocrat," his tall tale, maybe his tallest. On reflection, I realized I'd married him partly because I saw him as my ticket to the other side, legitimate WASPocracy. Now I wondered if maybe I was *his* ticket out. Maybe some devious code in his family scripture called for an occasional "exotic" marriage, offspring with a touch of spice, a little jazz in the tidepool of stagnant family genes. I stopped talking about my heritage, felt I'd forsaken it. Increasingly uncomfortable in my husband's world, I buried myself in writing and let the marriage slide. I meant to have children; I thought I did, but books came out instead. In the next four years I sold several stories and wrote two unpublishable novels.

I wasn't writing for pleasure then, and certainly it wasn't for the money. I think I was doing it because I was lost and extremely lonely and writing seemed to approximate the actions of someone jiggling a key in a lock, which would open a door that led me out of my condition. So I kept writing, jiggling the key, trying to engage all the tumblers. Here's a snapshot of me holding my divorce papers, and in the other hand a letter of acceptance from a publisher. After almost ten years of trying, I've finally sold a novel, and friends take me out to celebrate. I don't think about the divorce; reverberations will come in their time.

The novel was commercial and sold moderately well, and at a book-and-author luncheon I met a writer from Mississippi, a soft-spoken, courtly man, terribly attractive because he seemed to lack awe for anything. He took me home to one of those antebellum plantation houses with magnolia trees and mournful Spanish moss. I was charmed. Each night, we gathered on the front gallery, drinking with his friends—men in law and real estate, gentle with their women. I don't know when I started feeling uncomfortable. Maybe it was seeing Ruth, the black maid, slipping leftover food into her pocketbook. Or, it was the way Marcus, the black butler, served us. Tall, dignified, innate grace of a patriarch, he was over sixty. We should have been serving him.

One night my host and his friends got seriously into drink and telling jokes. As the jokes turned ugly, so did they, sounding like rednecks with calloused trigger fingers, sawed-off shotguns in their trucks. Each joke dragged a nail down the length of my spine. "A coon who st-st-stuttered . . ." "A nigger with such big lips, she could blow a man and smoke a Camel at the same time." All the while Ruth sat just inside the door, folding napkins. And all the while, Marcus served us drinks.

That night I woke with a jolt, my skin crackling, my heart trying to leap out of my chest. I dragged my suitcase down the stairs, packing in the dark. Marcus called a cab at dawn, before the house woke up, and waved me off, bewildered. On the plane back to New York I thought of an old snapshot, source of a young girl's nightmares. Men in white robes and cone-shaped hoods. That I had gotten out of there alive, survived brief truancy into the geography of that picture, seemed to me a miracle.

Years bucketed by. I published a second novel that quietly rolled over and died. The story I had hoped would absolutely scald, leave readers barking with shock and recognition, turned out to be a yawn. Insentient characters, anemic little lives. There was something I wasn't catching on to. I was still jiggling the key, still trying to engage the tumblers in that lock, but I couldn't open the door, couldn't get beyond that meta-physical place I was stuck in. What I hadn't yet learned was that a writer's voice is the sound of her convictions. Lack of conviction is the impulse of death; it sterilizes the writing. I hadn't scrutinized myself, still couldn't define who I was, what I stood for. I stopped fiction for a while, went back to writing about wigs and hair sprays.

One day I looked down, and when I looked up, my thirties were over. I understood that, very shortly, what I was, was what I would be from then on. Realizations didn't hit me all at once; some facts take hammering in. That summer I learned that a cousin in Honolulu had become a minister, another a lawyer. I'd missed their transitions, the celebrations. Then my favorite cousin, the one I loved most, the one whose letters I'd stopped answering, suddenly died. A nephew was fatally shot in the face. I'd missed most of their lives. After the paralyzing shock came grief, and I began to see that at a certain age life hits back, that the things we desert come after us.

One night at a cocktail party book launch on the twentieth floor of the Waldorf-Astoria, I glanced out of a window ex-pecting to see, far below, the YWCA. My shock was absolute. The Y and the entire block were gone, replaced by an eerie, massive crater, a prehistoric punchbowl surrounded by a tall makeshift construction fence. In two years another glass-and-chrome monolith would crowd the skyline. I thought of Meena and Sindiwa then, sad that we'd lost touch, and I wondered where they were, how their lives had fared.

Some months later, I read an article in the *Village Voice* on Nelson Mandela, with Sindiwa's byline. Her words leapt out, radiating passion. Yet her views against Apartheid were bal-anced, restrained, so her argument resonated beyond the mea-sure of the page. She traced me through my publisher, just as I was tracking her through the newspaper. We floated to each other down the avenue, laughing and crying out loud. Her Afro was very short, and she was wearing stiletto heels and a chic big-shouldered suit.

"Ah, yes, the dashikis, the turbans and beads. That is still my basic dress, but we need variety, no?" She hugged me over and over, squeezing my hands repeatedly. "Remember our gypsy rags? What did they call us? War Dolls! Wasn't it?"

She still had that forceful, physical glow, still full of incredible tremor. Hugging her, I could feel the surge. It had been over eighteen years, and we talked through dinner and far into the night. Sindiwa had spent several years on a Cleveland newspaper, then a year on the *Los Angeles Times*. She went home for two years and, one at a time, brought her children to New York. Now she free-lanced for liberal magazines and had written a book on South Africa, published in London. It won an award, and Meena, living in London, attended the ceremony. She had earned her law degree, married a diplomat, and went back and forth to New Delhi, torn between the new world and her own.

We talked about my novels, which Sindiwa had only recently discovered and read. She believed I had the true gift of a storyteller though I had not yet found my subject. She asked if I'd been home to the islands recently, then she looked at my face.

"I never went back," I said. "It's too late."

"It will happen." She took my hand. "It was hard for you, a half-caste. I used to watch you secretly. Your two selves, warring with each other."

The shock of it, of her knowing all those years ago, made me suddenly weep.

"Listen to me." She put her arm around me as if I were her very large child. "In my country, when whites stare at me, there's no ambiguity, it's pure hate. I always know who I am. You are different. Mixed blood, mixed cultures. You have to improvise, hide, take sides."

I talked about my marriage then, and the years of lying. I told her about my father's father, the Ku Klux Klan, how I was always aware that my cells contained that man's nuclei. How I had spent years ignoring my native blood, but ignoring the southern blood, too. It seemed I'd spent most of my life denying *all* of me, trying to run my genes off, like fat.

"Never mind," Sindiwa said. "We're all hybrids of the new world. Making ourselves up as we go along. This is why we write, juggling our little flames. One burns through muck to find the core."

We talked a lot in the next few months, and that summer I went home to Honolulu. My family was welcoming but wary, waiting to see what I'd become, if I'd become a mainland *haole*, the worst kind of white. I spent weeks getting my bearings, listening to aunties and uncles "talk story," retelling our family history. I lay on beaches with cousins and their kids, catching up on their lives, gossiped with old school friends and hiked ancient rain forests alone with a backpack. After a while, my family stepped closer, took me in completely, hugging, teasing, feeding me foods of my childhood: *saimin, mahi mahi, kimchi*, salty little silver-eyeballed fish.

Nieces pinched my arm, talking pidgin. "Plenty thin! You like *da kine poi*? More good for make you fat!" They wanted to find me a husband. "One local man, make good love for you."

Here's a snapshot of me surrounded by my clan, my *'ohana*. Tradewinds rustle banyans, blowing narcotic sizzle of ginger through the screens, while I talk about living on the island of Manhattan. Nephews listen with their mouths open, as if hearing fantastic tales of a shipwrecked sailor. For some things it's too late. My cousin died feeling I deserted her. She once wrote asking to visit New York, and I had made excuses. I sit beside her grave. I study my mother's photographs, stunned again by her early death. I think of my father.

One day, I started taking notes, tracing the line of our ancestors who, on my mother's mother's side, came to Hawai'i from Tahiti more than two thousand years ago, and the Dutchman on my mother's father's side, who rounded Cape Horn on a whaling ship in 1840 and sailed into the arms of a full-blooded Polynesian. The book will take several years to write. I don't rush it. I go home every summer now, swimming for hours in the Pacific. Back in New York, sometimes I dream I'm still swimming, and wake up with stiff arms, exhausted. Sometimes I feel I'm swimming through the city, stroking through crowds, a city now so multinational that not to be blonde and WASP is a bearable affliction.

Last year, Meena passed through New York and we had a reunion, meeting at the Waldorf for drinks. She still possessed that slender-boned beauty of a natural aristocrat, floating forward in bangled arms, a tangerine silk sari. Tears stood like jewels on her cheeks when we embraced. Sindiwa had reverted to the embodiment of the Ethnic Ideal—turban, dashiki, head to toe in bold colors, all dimmed by her dazzling smile. I was just back from the islands, a turquoise jumpsuit, orchid in my hair. We were who we were, no longer dressing like children wanting to mingle with the grown-ups.

Still the quiet renegade, no children, and drinking scotch, Meena was divorcing her husband and, for the present, remaining in London, helping legislate for more Indian women's crisis centers there. She felt there were enough children in the world, and rather than have her own, she said, one day she would adopt. We talked about this dual existence, our adopted cities versus our genesis, the conflicts and tension, the often comical struggle not to disappear into the "mainstream," the sense of accomplishment in holding fast to our identity through our work. At the moment, there were no men in our lives, and I wondered if that part of life was over.

Sindiwa responded in her wonderful Aframericanese. "Ladiees, please . . . it 'tisn't over . . .'til it's over, isn't it?"

We spent a great deal of that evening laughing, remembering the Y. The "house warden" discovering a pet monkey in a dress. A man discovered in someone's bed. Someone eloping, someone disappearing. Girls yelling back and forth from windows, like housewives beside a Chiang Mai *klong*. The ones the city rejected and the ones who left, rejecting the city instead. That night, after dinner, we strolled up the avenue past all-night Korean grocers and Senegalese hawking watches and scarves. Finally, we turned down the block where the Y should have been. A few boards were knocked out and we were able to look through the construction fence and down at the crater.

"War Doll Hotel," Meena said.

We were silent then, and the specter of that year, that place, floated up before us. Memories of the pluck and terror with which we arrived in the city almost twenty years ago, ready to trade in our identities in order to succeed, not knowing that the more we imitated New York, the more we lost the privilege of our uniqueness. That year never taught us all we expected it to. But it gave us an edge, made us alert, helped us understand that survival means the mind's, not the body's, ability to endure. The years in between taught us the rest, to keep one foot in the ideal plain of our origins.

Here's a snapshot of three friends laughing at the edge of a crater, like wondrous hybrid flowers, splashed palettes on the landscape.

'OHANA

Kubota

On December 8, 1941, the day after the Japanese attack on
Pearl Harbor in Hawaii, my grandfather barricaded himself
with his family—my grandmother, my teenage mother, her
two sisters and two brothers—inside his home in La'ie, a sugar
plantation village on Oahu's North Shore. This was my maternal grandfather, a man most villagers called by his last name—
Kubota. It could mean either "Wayside Field" or "Broken
Dreams," depending on which ideograms he used. Kubota ran
La'ie's general store, and the previous night, after a long day of
bad news on the radio, some locals had come by, pounded on
the front door, and made threats. One was said to have bran-
dished a machete. They were angry and shocked, as the whole
nation was, in the aftermath of the surprise attack. Kubota was
one of the few Japanese Americans in the village and president of the local Japanese language school. He had become a
target for their rage and suspicion. A wise man, he locked all
his doors and windows and did not open his store the next day,
but stayed closed and waited for news from some official.

He was a *Kibei*, a Japanese American born in Hawaii (a
United States territory then, so he was thus a citizen) and subsequently sent back by his father for formal education in Hiroshima, Japan—their home province. *Kibei* is written with two
ideograms in Japanese—one is the word for "return" and the
other is the word for "rice." Poetically, it means one who returns from America, known as the Land of Rice in Japanese (by
contrast, Chinese immigrants called their new home Mountain
of Gold).

Kubota was graduated from a Japanese high school and then

came back to Hawaii as a teenager. He spoke English—
a Hawaiian creole version of it at that—with a Japanes
cent. But he was well liked and good at numbers, scrupu
and hardworking like so many immigrants and children of
migrants. Castle and Cook, a grower's company that ran
sugar cane business along the North Shore, hired him on, first
as a stock-boy and then appointed him to run one of its company stores. He did well, gained the trust of management and
labor—not an easy accomplishment in any day—married, had
children, and had begun to exert himself in community affairs and excel in his own recreations. He put together a Japanese community organization that backed a Japanese language
school for children and sponsored teachers from Japan. Kubota
boarded many of them, in succession, in his own home. This
made dinners a silent affair for his talkative, Hawaiian-bred
children, as their stern *sensei*, or teacher, was nearly always at
table and their own abilities in the Japanese language were as
delinquent as their attendance. While Kubota and the *sensei*
rattled on about things Japanese, speaking Japanese, his children hurried through supper and tried to run off early to listen
to the radio shows.

After dinner, while the *sensei* graded exams seated in a
wicker chair in the spare room and his wife and children
gathered around the radio in the front parlor, Kubota sat on
the screened porch outside, reading the local Japanese newspapers. He finished reading about the same time as he finished the tea he drank for his digestion—a habit he'd learned
in Japan—and then he'd get out his fishing gear and spread it
out on the plank floors. The wraps on his rods needed to be re-
done, gears in his reels needed oil, and once through with those
tasks, he'd painstakingly wind on hundreds of yards of new
line. Fishing was his hobby and his passion. He spent weekends camping along the North Shore beaches with his children,
setting up umbrella tents, packing a rice pot and hibachi along

for meals. And he caught fish. *Ulu'a* mostly, the huge surf-feeding fish known as jack crevalle on the Mainland, but he'd go after almost anything in its season. In Kawela, a plantation-owned bay nearby, he fished for mullet Hawaiian style with a throw net, stalking the bottom-hugging, gray-backed schools as they gathered at the stream mouths and in the freshwater springs. In an outrigger out beyond the reef, he'd try for *aku*— the skipjack tuna prized for steaks and, sliced raw and mixed with fresh seaweed and cut onions, for *sashimi* salad. In Kaha-luu and Ka'awa and on an offshore rock locals called Goat Island, he loved to go torching, stringing lanterns on bamboo poles stuck in the sand to attract *kumu'u*, the red goatfish, as they schooled at night just inside the reef. But in La'ie on Lani-loa Point near Kahuku, the northernmost tip of Oahu, he cast twelve- and fourteen-foot surf rods for the huge, varicolored, fast-running *ulu'a* as they ran for schools of squid and baitfish just beyond the biggest breakers and past the low sand flats wadable from the shore to nearly a half mile out. At sunset, against the western light, he looked as if he were walking on water as he came back, fish and rods slung over his shoulders, stepping along the rock and coral path just inches under the surface of a running tide.

When it was torching season, in December or January, he'd drive out the afternoon before and stay with old friends, the Tanakas or the Yoshikawas, shopkeepers like him who ran stores near the fishing grounds. They'd have been preparing for weeks, selecting and cutting their bamboo poles, cleaning the hurricane lanterns, tearing up burlap sacks for the cloths they'd soak with kerosene and tie onto sticks they'd poke into the soft sand of the shallows. Once lit, touched off with a Zippo lighter, these would be the torches they'd use as beacons to attract the schooling fish. In another time, they might have made up a dozen paper lanterns of the kind mostly used for decorating the summer folk dances outdoors on the grounds of the Buddhist church during *O-Bon*, the Festival for the Dead. But now, wealthy and modern and efficient killers of fish, Tanaka and Kubota used rag torches and Colemans and cast rods with tips made of Tonkin bamboo and butts of American-spun fiberglass. After just one good night they might bring back a prize bounty of a dozen burlap bags filled with scores of bloody, rigid fish delicious to eat and even better to give away as gifts to friends, family, and special customers.

It was a Monday night, the day after Pearl Harbor, and there was a rattling knock at the front door. Two FBI agents presented themselves, showed identification, and took my grandfather in for questioning in Honolulu. No one knew what had happened or what was wrong. But there was a roundup of all those in the Japanese-American community suspected of sympathizing with the enemy and worse. My grandfather was suspected of espionage, of communicating with offshore Japanese submarines launched from the attack fleet days before the attack. Torpedo planes and escort fighters, decorated with the insignia of the rising sun, had taken an approach route from northwest of Oahu directly across Kahuku Point and on toward Pearl. They had strafed an auxiliary air station near the fishing grounds my grandfather loved and destroyed a small gun battery there, killing three men. Kubota was known to have sponsored and harbored Japanese nationals in his own home. He had a radio. He had wholesale access to firearms. Circumstances and an undertone of racial resentment had combined with wartime hysteria in the aftermath of the tragic naval battle to cast suspicion on the loyalties of my grandfather and all other Japanese Americans. The FBI reached out and pulled in hundreds of them for questioning in dragnets cast throughout the West Coast and Hawaii.

My grandfather was lucky, he was released after only a few days. But others were not as fortunate. Hundreds, from small communities in Washington, California, Oregon, and Hawaii, were rounded up and, after what appeared to be routine questioning, shipped off under Justice Department orders to holding centers in Leuppe on the Navajo Reservation in Arizona, in Fort Missoula in Montana, and on Sand Island in Honolulu Harbor. There were other special camps, on Maui in Ha'iku, and on Hawaii—the Big Island—in my own home village of Volcano.

Many of these men—it was exclusively Japanese-American men suspected of ties to Japan who were initially rounded up—did not see their families again for more than four years. Under a suspension of due process that was only after the fact ruled as warranted by military necessity, they were, if only temporarily, "disappeared" in Justice Department prison camps scattered in particularly desolate areas of the United States designated as militarily "safe." These were grim forerunners to the assembly centers and concentration camps for the 120,000 Japanese-American evacuees who were to come later.

Or, because I want so badly to belong to the main story, to the history of Japanese in America, I tell myself that Kubota was *not* lucky. I tell myself he was taken to a detention center on Sand Island in Honolulu Harbor, kept there while he awaited interrogation from the FBI and other federal officials sent by the Justice Department to assess the sabotage and fifth column activity that was suspected. I say he ate military food and slept in street clothes. I decide he had no contact with his family, no way to get them word that he was all right. He slept on a canvas cot in a *kamaboko* hut—an oval-roofed military shack shaped like a Japanese fish cake. For days he marched out with the others every morning for inspection, exercise, a group march to the commissary. They saw American fighter planes and transports flying overhead, a few ships and tugs churning through the harbor, carriers steaming far away beyond the breakwater. They gossiped about the war, the foolishness of Japan, the panic of the day Pearl Harbor was bombed.

"News come, everybody running!" said a man from Makiki. "My boy jump on his bike. He was going go A'ala Park, watch fire engine and ambulance! What kine kid dat, eh? I had to grab him off it—I didn't want him get killed!"

"Yeah, we saw plane after plane flying overhead that morning—vee after vee in formation, waves of them," said Tanaka of Kahuku, the village near Kubota's. "And I thought, what strange kine maneuvers this! We was outside, cleaning yard, gazing up at the sky, picking papayas in the side patch by the house. How could *we* know?"

Kubota was silent. He wanted to play cards, to sit around after mess and tell stories as he used to back in his store in La'ie, but he said nothing to anyone. The war changed everything, and he felt it deeply. Things had gotten terribly strange. After a week, he was interviewed by an agent, then by another agent, then by the first agent again. Each time, the questions were the same—*Where were you born? Why did you leave Hawaii? What kind of school did you attend in Hiroshima? Do you believe the Japanese emperor is a god?* He gave each question the same answer. "I am citizen," Kubota said, "American-born."

America raged and hunted for victims. *Washington Post* columnist Walter Lippmann claimed that American Japs had directed the dive bombers across the mountains and cane fields to Pearl. "It is a fact that communication takes place between the enemy at sea and enemy agents on land," he wrote. Military and government officials on the West Coast called for the mass incarceration of the entire Japanese-American population on the grounds that they were "an enemy race" or, at the very least, that enemy agents lurked among them. Suspected of being one of these, Kubota was interrogated again and again; then, after others had been released back to their families, he was led off, in handcuffs, to a steamship bound for Oakland, California.

Back at home in La'ie, my grandmother did not immediately panic. She conferred with her family in Kahuku, almost a clan, they numbered so many, and word came back that many of the elders and community leaders—mostly Japan-born—had been arrested and then released. Surely Kubota, an American-born, would be coming home soon. Meanwhile, she took in washing and ironing, did some sewing for the ladies from the Mormon church, and waited for Kubota to come home.

He did not. In this story that I tell you and that I tell myself in order to belong to the history of America, I say Kubota was sent from Oakland to Fort Missoula, a military post in western Montana, and held there for some months. He was kept for some time in the jail, and he whiled away the boredom making up songs and poems. At first he wrote *senryu*, those seventeen-syllable satirical haiku. "Winter in the yard . . . ," one said, "The camp dog howls at night . . . And the Japanese by day." Or he would contrast his memories of the snowfall in Hiroshima with the snowfall in Missoula: "Japan winter—snow and plum blossoms; Montana's—snow and stinging dust." Later, he'd compose whole songs as he tramped through another drill on the exercise yard. He'd hear a cowboy song from the guards and make up Japanese words for it. "Laredo" seemed to him like an old sake-drinking dirge he'd learned in a card room back in Hiroshima. He changed the cowboy to a coal miner, the gunshot to a crucifix from the miner's dead lover. And he mixed languages, shouting "Santa Maria!" at song's end. The miner confessing his love was Christian and Caucasian—a Catholic from Portugal, and *not* Japanese. It was a tragedy. And Kubota laughed to sing it. "Santa Maria!" he sang in the yard, and he'd gaze upward toward the guards in the towers shouldering their rifles and cleaning the machine guns.

My grandmother took in laundry for others on the plantation now, foremen and clerks in the office. I heard a story that she fell in love with someone, a man named di Regis or del

Riggio, a man from the Mainland, New Jersey or Pennsylvania, a nice man with curly hair, and he gave her a child, a girl. In the middle year of the war, after the American flight from the Philippines, after the fall of Corrigedor, and after the turning of the tide with our naval victory at Midway at the end of the Hawaiian chain of islands, my grandmother carried a child to term, wondering how to endure the humiliation, what had become of her husband, what to do with her feelings for her lover. She buried everything in a story. She thought of bundling the infant in blankets and then leaving her under the stand of ironwood trees on the short Jeep road leading off the highway, through the village, down to Kahuku Point. That was where her own mother had been assigned to go the two times she adopted the bastard children of others in the village. She had a foundling sister called "Pine Woman," after the circumstances of the adoption. She had a foundling brother, a full-blood Hawaiian named "Seaweed Boy" after the drift-weeds and kelp piled on the beach where he was found. My grandmother washed and sewed and cooked and dreamed of many things to do with her new baby, but it was decided by her clan that she should give the child away to relatives on Molokai. Though these were not childless people, they prospered and had plenty to go around. The father worked for the military base, got fairly high up, and so could raise the girl and give her another history no one around would care to dispute. He spoke English well, got along with the whites, and, a judo man, he was ferocious among the Japanese. And they were on another island. The girl would grow up without having to hear conflicting stories of her birth.

"It was wartime," a cousin or an aunt said, telling me this story, "and nobody knew what happened, where your grandfather was, what the world was coming to. We just let it go and tried to help each other."

Six months went by, still with no word, and I decide Kubota

was sent to Arizona, to a prison on the Navajo nation at a trading post near Flagstaff called Leuppe, a crossroads in the middle of sheep and hogan country. He went by train and truck, then bus and Jeep. He was again placed in a stockade, but this one was out in the open, off by itself across from the trading post and Indian schoolhouse he could see from the cell window. It was like a jail in the movie westerns starring Irishman George O'Brien and Hawaiian sidekick Duke Kahanamoku. Dirt floor, log-and-chinked adobe walls, a steel-mesh bench suspended from the walls by two thick iron chains.

Kubota would be there a week, be interrogated yet again, then be released from the cell to walk about the compound almost as a free man. He'd be given jobs—sweeping up in the trading post, cleaning out the stables, then cooking for the camp mess (a job he liked because it kept his mind and body busiest and gave him the appreciation of his guards and fellows). He couldn't run away—Leuppe was fourteen miles along a dirt road from the crossroads to Flagstaff, another ten miles down the highway. If he ran off across the chaparral and sheep shit, he might come across a Navajo's abandoned hogan after ten miles, but that was all. The San Francisco peaks blocked his way west, the Painted Desert and red Kachina Cliffs cut him off north, and, after the slow roll of the Colorado Plateau toward the Mogollon Rim, there was the nearly infinite Sonoran Desert spreading away to the south. If he went east, he'd run into gullies, then canyons, then a pinyon forest, then pine and fir forests and the Hopi buttes, then mountains, and then finally another desert, this one almost completely dry.

Kubota cooked and rummaged about, using army and Bureau of Indian Affairs supplies. He made a Navajo sukiyaki out of mutton scraps, chopped onions, pinyon nuts, a jigger of Four Roses, and lots of garlic. After a while, the guards let him mingle more, and Kubota traded food for Navajo clay—spoons and pots, a jug for water—and a military-size mayonnaisse jar for collecting colored stones. He liked the crystals and quartzes the best, and also the ambers, obsidians, and the petrified woods, preferring all of them even to the turquoise the Indians valued, and saw they were the stone flowers, anemones, and corals from an ancient sea. He built his mind up and let the past in as a story he'd allow himself to enter again the day he returned to his store in La'ie. The desert was like an ocean, the mountains like clouds over the sea. After three years the Justice Department sent him home. By then he needed nothing as a reward, and he told no tales to anyone of where he'd been. Empty of riches and without regard for them, he decided there was nothing to pass along.

When he returned, the world was almost as different from what he'd known as the prison camps had been. Many of his Japanese things had disappeared or been broken, his books thrown away, the lacquer *butsudan* he'd had shipped from Hiroshima moved from its place in the parlor into a bedroom. It was used now to store photographs, army surplus chocolate, and tins of dehydrated cream. On its shelves were no incense sticks or images of the Buddha. And though the bell bowl was still seated on its red pillow, he could not ring it for the chanting of sutras because inside, where it should have been empty as the heart/mind, there was instead a mound of copper-and-zinc pennies like a pyramind of chicken dung. His wife had wept when he returned. She came to him when the army Jeep pulled up and dropped him off, dropping her gift and running up the dirt road like a schoolgirl and wearing a red hibiscus in her black hair, but Kubota looked around the house and saw that his oldest child, a son, had kept nothing alive while he was gone. His pets and collection of dwarf pines were all dead, given away, or traded for food. The boy, now eighteen, had become delinquent, a gambler; he flaunted his illiteracy in Japanese as much as he liked flaunting a GI style of dress and smoking cigarettes. He was "cool" and blew smoke rings as he took a pose leaning against a wall, rattling dice with a hand stuffed deep into his pants pocket. Bereft even of anger, Kubota could not hit him. He turned away.

"Your body is *hard*, Papa," his wife said to him in bed that night.

"Your body hard too," Kubota said.

"The war make it hard," she answered, and they were silent for a long time, awake in bed, their breathing not together.

Kubota tried to fall back into his old life, yet his children raised themselves now, and his wife was slow to come to him. For the longest while, despite all the strangeness, he was outwardly made only the slightest shade more grim.

I am Kubota's eldest grandchild, and I remember him as a lonely, habitually silent old man who lived with us in our home near Los Angeles for most of my childhood and adolescence. It was the 1950s, and my parents had emigrated from Hawaii to the Mainland in the hope of a better life away from the old sugar plantation. After some success, they had sent for my grandparents and taken them in. And it was my grandparents who did the work of the household while my mother and father worked their salaried city jobs. My grandmother cooked and sewed, washed our clothes, and knitted in the front room under the light of a huge lamp with a bright three-way bulb. Kubota raised a flower garden, read up on soils and grasses in gardening books, and planted a zoysia lawn in front and a dichondra one in back. He planted a small patch near the rear wall with green onions, eggplants, white Japanese radishes, and cucumbers. While he hoed and spaded the loamless, clayey earth of Los Angeles, he sang particularly plangent songs in Japanese about plum blossoms and bamboo groves.

Once, in the mid-1960s, after a dinner during which, as always, he had been silent while he worked away at a meal of fish and rice spiced with dabs of Chinese mustard and catsup thinned with soy sauce, Kubota took his own dishes to the kitchen sink and washed them. He took a clean jelly jar out of the cupboard—the glass was thick and its shape squatty like an old-fashioned—and reached around to the hutch below, where he kept his bourbon. He made himself a drink and retired to the living room, where I was expected to join him for "talk story"—the Hawaiian idiom for "chewing the fat."

I was a teenager and, though I was bored listening to stories I'd heard often enough before at holiday dinners, I was dutiful. I took my spot on the couch next to Kubota and heard him out. Usually, he'd tell me about his schooling in Japan, where he learned judo along with mathematics and literature. He'd learned the *soroban* there—the abacus that was the original pocket calculator of the Far East—and that, along with his strong, judo-trained back, got him his first job in Hawaii. This was the moral. "Study *ha-ahd*," he'd say with pidgin emphasis. "Learn read good. Learn speak da kine *good* English." The message is the familiar one taught to any children of immigrants: succeed through education. And imitation. But this time Kubota reached down into his past and told me a different story. I was thirteen by then, and I suppose he thought me ready for it. He told me about Pearl Harbor, how the planes flew in formations, wing after wing, over his old house in La'ie in Hawaii, and how, the next day, after Roosevelt had made his famous "Day of Infamy" speech about the treachery of the Japanese, the FBI agents had come to his door and taken him in, hauled him off to Honolulu for questioning and held him without charge. I thought he was lying. I thought he was making up a kind of horror story to shock me and give his moral that much more starch. But it was true. I asked around. I brought it up during history class in junior high school and my teacher, after silencing me and stepping me off to the back of the room, told me that it was indeed so. I asked my mother and she said it was true. I asked my schoolmates, who laughed and ridiculed me for being so ignorant. We lived in a Japanese-American community, and the parents of most of my class-mates were the Nisei who had been interned as teenagers all through the war. But there was a strange silence around all of this. There was a hush, as if one were invoking the ill powers of the dead when one brought it up. No one cared to speak about the evacuation and relocation for very long. It wasn't in our his-tory books, though we were studying World War II at the time. It wasn't in the family albums of the people I knew and visited, staying over weekends with friends. And it wasn't anything that the family talked about or allowed me to keep bringing up, either. I was given the facts, told sternly and pointedly that "it was war" and that "nothing could be done." *Shikatta ga nai* is the phrase in Japanese, a kind of resolute and determin-ist pronouncement on how to deal with inexplicable tragedy. I was to know it but not to dwell on it. Japanese Americans were busy trying to forget it ever happened and were having a hard enough time building their new lives after "camp." It was as if we had no history for four years and the relocation was something unspeakable.

But Kubota would not let it go. In session after session, for months it seemed, he pounded away at his story. He wanted to tell me the names of the FBI agents. He went over their questions and his responses again and again. He'd tell me how one would try to act friendly toward him, offering him cigarettes while the other, who hounded him with accusa-tions and threats, left the interrogation room. "Good cop/bad cop," I thought to myself, already superficially streetwise from stories black classmates told of the Watts riots and from my-self having watched too many episodes of "Dragnet" and "The Mod Squad." But Kubota was not interested in my experi-ences. I was not made yet, and he was determined that his stories be part of my making. He spoke quietly at first, mildly, but once into his narrative and after his drink was down his voice would rise and quaver with resentment and he'd make his accusations. He gave his testimony to me and I held it at first cautiously in my conscience like it was an heirloom too delicate to expose to strangers and anyone outside the world Kubota made with his words. "I give you story now," he once said, "and you learn speak good, eh?" It was my job, as the disciple of his preaching I had then become, Ananda to his Buddha, to reassure him with a promise. "You learn speak good like the Dillingham," he said another time, referring to the wealthy scion of the grower family who had once run, un-successfully, for one of Hawaii's first senatorial seats. Or he'd invoke a magical name, the name of one of his heroes, a man he thought particularly exemplary and righteous. "Learn speak dah good Ing-rish like *Mistah Inouye*," Kubota shouted. "He *lick* dah Dillingham even in debate. I saw on *terre-bision* my-self." He was remembering the debates before the first senato-rial election just before Hawaii was admitted to the Union as its fiftieth state. "You *tell* story," Kubota would end. And I had my injunction.

The town we settled in after the move from Hawaii is called Gardena, the independently incorporated city south of Los Angeles and north of San Pedro harbor. As its northern limit it borders on Watts and Compton—black towns. To the south-west are Torrance and Redondo Beach—white towns. To the rest of Los Angeles, Gardena is primarily famous for having legalized five-card draw poker after the war. On Vermont Boulevard, its eastern border, there is a dingy little Vegas-like strip of card clubs with huge parking lots and flickering neon signs that spell out "The Rainbow" and "The Horseshoe" in timed sequences of varicolored lights. The town is only second-arily famous as the largest community of Japanese Americans in the United States outside Honolulu, Hawaii.

When I was in high school there, it seemed to me that every Sansei kid I knew wanted to be a doctor, an engineer, or a pharmacist. Our fathers were gardeners or electricians or nurserymen or ran small businesses catering to other Japanese Americans. Our mothers worked in civil service for the city or as cashiers for Thrifty Drug. What the kids wanted was a good job, good pay, a fine home, and no troubles. No one wanted to mess with the law—from either side—and no one wanted to mess with language or art. They all talked about getting into the right clubs so that they could go to the right schools. There was a certain kind of sameness, an intensely enforced system of conformity. Style was all. Boys wore moccasin-sewn shoes from Flagg Brothers, black A-1 slacks, and Kensington shirts with high collars. Girls wore their hair up in stiff bouffants solidified in hairspray and knew all the latest dances from the slauson to the funky chicken. We did well in chemistry and in math; no other Japanese but me spoke in English class or in history unless called upon, and no one talked about World War II. The day after Robert Kennedy was assassinated after winning the California Democratic Primary, we worked on calculus and elected class coordinators for the prom, featuring the Fifth Dimension. We avoided grief. We avoided government. We avoided strong feelings and dangers of any kind. Once punished, we tried to maintain a concerted emotional and social discipline and would not willingly seek to fall outside the narrow margin of protective favor again.

But when I was thirteen, in junior high, I'd not understood why it was so difficult for my classmates, those who were themselves Japanese American, to talk about the relocation. They had cringed, too, when I tried to bring it up during our discussions of World War II. I was Hawaiian-born. They were Mainland-born. Their parents had been in camp, had been the ones to suffer the complicated experience of having to distance themselves from their own history and all things Japanese in order to make their way back into the American social and economic mainstream. It was out of this sense of shame and a fear of stigma, I was only beginning to understand, that the Nisei had silenced themselves. And for their children, among whom I grew up, they wanted no heritage, no culture, no contact with a defiled history. I recall the silence very well. The Japanese-American children around me were burdened in a way I was not. Their injunction was silence. Mine was to speak.

Away at college, in another protected world in its own way as magical to me as the Hawaii of my childhood, I dreamed about my grandfather. Tired from studying languages, practicing German conjugations or scripting an army's worth of Chinese ideograms on a single sheet of paper, Kubota would come to me as I drifted off into sleep. Or I would have walked across the newly mown ballfield in back of my dormitory, cutting through a street-side phalanx of ancient eucalyptus trees on my way to visit friends off-campus, and I would think of him, his anger, and his sadness.

I don't know myself what makes someone feel that kind of need to have a story they've lived through be deposited somewhere, but I can guess. I think about *The Iliad, The Odyssey, The Peloponnesian Wars* of Thucydides, and the myriad works of literature I've studied. A character—almost a *topoi*, he occurs so often—is frequently the witness who gives personal testimony about an event the rest of his community cannot even imagine. The Sibyl is such a character; and Procne, the maid whose tongue is cut out so that she will not tell that she has been raped by her own brother-in-law, the king of Thebes. There are the dime novels and the epic blockbusters Hollywood makes into miniseries, and then there are the plain, relentless stories of witnesses who have suffered through horrors major and minor that have marked and changed their lives. I haven't talked to Holocaust victims. But I've read their survival stories and their stories of witness and been revolted and moved by them. My father-in-law tells me his war stories again and again and I listen. A Mennonite who set aside the strictures of his own church in order to serve, he was a marine code man in the Pacific during World War II, in the signal corps on Guadalcanal, Morotai, and Bougainville. He was part of the island-hopping maneuver MacArthur had devised to win the war in the Pacific. He saw friends die from bombs that exploded not ten yards away. When he was with 298th Signal Corps attached to the 13th Air Force, he saw plane after plane come in and crash, just short of the runway, killing their crews, setting the jungle ablaze with oil and gas fires. Emergency wagons would scramble, bouncing over newly bulldozed land men had used just the afternoon before for a football game. Every time we go fishing together, whether it's in a McKenzie boat drifting for salmon in Tillamook Bay or taking a lunch break from wading the riffles of a stream in the Cascades, my father-in-law tells me about what happened to him and the young men in his unit. One was a Jewish boy from Brooklyn. One was a foul-mouthed kid from Kansas. They died. And he *has* to tell me. And I *have* to listen. It's a ritual payment the young owe their elders who have survived. The evacuation and relocation is something like that.

Kubota, my grandfather, had been ill with Alzheimer's disease for some time before he died. At the house he'd built on Kamehameha Highway in Hau'ula, a seacoast village just down the road from La'ie, where he had his store, he'd wander out from the garage or greenhouse where he'd set up a workbench, and trudge down to the beach or up toward the line of pines he'd planted while employed by the Works Project Administration during the 1930s. Kubota thought he was going fishing. Or he thought he was back at work for Roosevelt planting pines as a wind- or soilbreak on the windward flank of the Ko'olau Mountains, emerald monoliths rising out of sea and cane fields from Wailua to Kaneohe. When I visited, my grandmother would send me down to the beach to fetch him. Or I'd run down Kam Highway a quarter mile or so and find him hiding in the cane field by the roadside, counting stalks, measuring circumferences in the claw of his thumb and forefinger. The look on his face was confused or concentrated—I didn't know which. But I guessed he was going fishing again. I'd grab him and walk him back to his house on the highway. My grandmother would shut him in a room.

Within a few years, Kubota had a stroke and survived it, then he had another one and was completely debilitated. The family decided to put him in a nursing home in Kahuku, set just back from the highway within a mile or so of Kahuku Point and the Tanaka Store where he had his first job as a stockboy. He lived there three years, and I visited him once with my aunt. He was like a potato that had been worn down by cooking. Everything on him—his eyes, his teeth, his legs and torso—seemed like it had been sloughed away. What he had been was mostly gone now, and I was looking at the nub of a man. In a wheelchair, he grasped my hands and tugged on them—violently. His hands were still thick and, I believed, strong enough to lift me out of my own seat and into his lap. He murmured something in Japanese—he'd long ago ceased to speak any English. My aunt and I cried a little, and we left him.

I remember walking out on the black asphalt of the parking lot of the nursing home. It was heat-cracked and eroded already, and grass had veined itself into the interstices. There were coconut trees around, a cane field across the street, and the ocean, I knew, was pitching a surf just beyond it. The green Ko'olaus rose up behind us. Somewhere nearby, alongside the beach, there was an abandoned airfield in the middle of the canes. As a child, I'd come upon it playing one day, and my friends and I kept returning to it, day after day, playing war or sprinting games or flying kites. I recognize it even now when I see it on TV—it's used as a site for action scenes in the detective shows Hollywood sets in the Islands: a helicopter chasing the hero racing away in a Ferrari, or gun dealers making a clandestine rendezvous on the abandoned runway. It was the old airfield strafed by Japanese planes the day the major flight attacked Pearl Harbor. It was the airfield the FBI thought my grandfather had targeted in his night fishing and was signaling with the long surfpoles he'd stuck in the sandy bays near Kahuku Point.

Kubota died a short while after I visited him, but not, I thought, without giving me a final message. I was on the Mainland, in California studying for Ph.D. exams, when my grandmother called me with the news. It was a relief. He'd suffered from his debilitation a long time, and I was grateful he was gone. I went home for the funeral and gave the eulogy. My grandmother and I took his ashes home in a small, heavy, metal box wrapped in a black *furoshiki*—a large, silk scarf. She showed me the name the priest had given to him on his death, scripted with a calligraphy brush on a long, narrow talent of plain wood. Buddhist commoners, at death, are given priestly names and received symbolically into the clergy. The idea is that in their next life, one of scholarship and leisure, they might meditate and attain the enlightenment the religion is aimed at. *Shaku Shūchi*, the ideograms read. It was Kubota's Buddhist name, incorporating characters from his family and given names. It means "Shining Wisdom of the Law." He died on Pearl Harbor Day, December 7, 1983.

After years, after I'd finally come back to live in Hawaii again, only once did I dream of Kubota, my grandfather. It was the same night I'd heard that HR 442, the redress bill for Japanese Americans, had been signed into law. In my dream that night Kubota was torching, and he sang a Japanese song, a querulous and wavery folk ballad, as he hung paper lanterns on bamboo poles stuck into the sand in the shallow water of the lagoon behind the reef near Kahuku Point. Then he was at a worktable, smoking a hand-rolled cigarette, letting it dangle from his lips Bogart style as he drew, daintily and skillfully,

with a narrow trim brush, ideogram after ideogram on a score
of paper lanterns he had hung in a dark shed to dry. He had
painted a talismanic mantra onto each lantern, the ideogram
for the word *red* in Japanese, a bit of art blended with some
superstition, a piece of sympathetic magic appealing to the
magenta coloring on the rough skins of the schooling, night-
feeding fish he wanted to attract to his baited hooks. He strung
them from pole to pole in the dream then, hiking up his khaki
work pants so his white ankles showed and wading through the
shimmering black waters of the sand flats and then the reef.
"The moon is leaving, leaving," he sang in Japanese. "Take
me deeper in the savage sea." He turned and crouched like
an ice racer then, leaning forward so that his unshaven face
almost touched the light film of water. I could see the light
stubble of beard like a fine, gray ash covering the lower half
of his face. I could see his gold-rimmed spectacles. He held a
small wooden boat in his cupped hands and placed it lightly
on the sea and pushed it away. One of his lanterns was on it,
and, written in small, neat rows like a sutra scroll, it had been
decorated with the silvery names of all our dead.

Jiddo: A Portrait

Over a period of years, I kept notes for a fragmented memoir of my Lebanese grandfather and my life in Lebanon. Memories are so elusive, so easy to alter, that I actually disguised the memoir, put it in the form of fiction. Its accuracies are often emotional rather than factual—the names are changed, except, of course, the name of Jiddo, which means "grandfather" in Arabic. This seemed to be the best way to express the feeling of distance and separation one experiences when one has left one world for another. (In the last days in the old place one has already departed and in the first days in the new place one is constantly returning.) I have never stopped returning.

This is really a story of the last time I saw Lebanon, and it contains my last "real" images of the country. All the images that followed, in the years after leaving, have been drawn/invented by others. But *this* is my final vision—a farewell glance at a life and a person soon to be relegated to the box of the past. This is not to say that my grandfather and his culture do not play a tremendously important role in my current life. My experience in Lebanon informs many waking moments and dreams—it certainly affects my vision of the American world that surrounds me. Often when I stride down New York City's trash-ridden streets I imagine that I am trudging up an ancient road, through a dusty village in the Lebanese mountains . . . Those images will stay with me forever. They make me *hungry* for the sea and the mountains and the marketplaces and tiled courtyards. The straight lines and uniform colors of urban America often do not please . . . They make me crave something else—some other values: a culture where an old and respected man spent hours telling stories to his grandchildren and walking in the mountains. A culture where age and wisdom seemed to be worth something . . .

Unfortunately, it is too easy to idealize from afar, to invent a portrait of a Middle Eastern Camelot. If Jiddo's wisdom had truly been heeded, Lebanon would not have suffered so many years of civil war. Although he did not manage to transform the world, he *did* transform (over years) my own sense of life and history. He was a gentleman (in the best sense of the word), a scholar, and a storyteller. Above all, he taught me to value and never try to avoid the *time* it takes to learn and do something well. And also the *value* of doing it well—and that this value has nothing to do with money. He taught this by example and metaphor, by the disciplined and rational way he lived his life. He never preached. As a child I was often a bit of a brat, and he taught me something about dignity and tolerance, about the value of hard work whether or not it is recognized. He taught me never to feign ignorance or knowledge and to continually educate my own heart and mind, and those of others. For me, his very *being* proved that principles and ideals are as crucial to daily life as food or air or water. When I think of him, I am given the strength to uphold those principles and ideals even when I am not encouraged to do so.

There is now a sadness that runs through my daily life—the knowledge that I have lost a place and person I loved dearly but knew only partially. This causes a *double* sense of loss— for what was and for what could have been. What is so often lost when one comes here, to the United States, is the sense of history and community so naturally provided by the extended family structure, with the grandfather at its head. Recently I attended my cousin's wedding in North Carolina and partook again, for a poignant and fleeting moment, of the richness and comfort of the larger family unit. We were all captured together

in Greenville for a few days before we dispersed geographically
and ethnically . . .

The war was too much for him, they said. He did not care
to leave his country even when it was hell to be there, and
when he finally agreed to leave, for the sake of his shell-
shocked, high-strung wife, he died in his sleep. He would remember the country as it had been—a masterwork of diplo-
macy where hundreds of sects lived in peaceful cohabitation.
As they bragged in the tourist brochures, *Fly to Lebanon, a
land of plenty, you can do just as you please there, no one will
interfere. What Paradise. What Possibility.*

But the war was too much for him. For one thing, he could
no longer take slow walks through the mountains. It was too
dangerous and he was constantly monitored by his nervous
wife, a matriarch gone sour—proper, shrewish, and elderly,
even though she was thirty years younger than he. When they
were in Beirut he was not allowed outside. He settled the matter by walking around the huge dining room table and up and
down the balcony all day long. When his granddaughter came
to visit, she followed him, bewildered and dizzy, as he told her
stories of his childhood in the mountains. They called him a
crazy old man behind his back, a stubborn fool. Even when the
bullets whizzed by, he continued to walk rhythmically along
the rail of the balcony. The war would break his heart, so he
refused to see it. He continued to live as he could, in the way
he knew.

He was not a man to make a fuss. His patience drew admiration and also the occasional scorn of his favorite granddaughter, Jumana. She wanted him to rebel against the tyranny of
her grandmother Marie and lured him to take long walks in
the mountains. When Marie insisted that he limit his wanderings to one hour, the scheming granddaughter insisted on a
two-hour adventure.

What more can one say of a grandfather one barely knew? A granddaughter, deprived of his stories by his sudden death, tries to imagine what his life was made of.

He was a rebel from the start, although he chose to live under the disguise of reason. As a boy he left school because the Jesuit priests beat him. He escaped to a neighboring village and found a Protestant missionary school where education seemed to be more than a sore derriere.

As a young man he walked daily from his mountain village to Beirut to attend university. His pace was slow and steady and he ambled up and down the hills, deep in thought.

As an old man he told Jumana stories with gestures of the hands. It was not his words that fascinated her but his hands, poised in the air, ready to talk. Mostly the stories were ordinary, about little girls in red capes who tromped through the woods to eat fried eggs and bread with their respectable grandmothers.

The memories are dim, no different from most memories of grandfathers in one's childhood. But there was something so methodical about him.

He was forty-five when he found his bride; she was fifteen, a beautiful young girl living in Damascus under the protection of a stern father who kept her in the house all day, safe from the eyes of the world. She learned to play the piano, she learned French and mathematics, and she cultivated the charm and wit she was born with. He had been upgrading himself for twenty years so that he would be worthy of a fine and lovely wife. His seriousness and learning bewildered her, for she was young, a spirited girl who knew little of life or hard work. She was not a scholar.

He took her to New York, where he studied mathematics and she lived in isolation, bloated with her first child. When they returned to Beirut their eldest son was born, expected to bring them honor and comfort from the day of his birth. He obediently became a brilliant young man and traveled to America to study science. When he came home she inundated him with his favorite foods:

"No, Mama, I've had enough."

"But you must eat more. I made you more."

"I'm not hungry."

"You don't love me! Take this food, take it from my hand. From my hand!"

"From my hand!" she shrieked as he stalked away from the table.

His father watched this with an air of detached amusement, knowing that they had lost their son to the Western world. In the West, he knew, they did not offer food three times at one meal. One ate and was finished with it. In the West, he concluded, there was no drama at the dinner table. Food symbolized nothing where his son had been—it was necessary and often bland nutrition. Lives were not dominated by cooking and food, as his wife's life was. The feeding of her children gave her energy and direction and an overwhelming sense of purpose. Nothing was so horrible to her as a child who refused food. He smiled at his raging wife, thinking all the while that she had become quite heavy.

"The boy must eat!" she screamed at him. "He will not eat! He is so thin, he looks American."

He smiled again, peering at her from the top of his heavy book. "Leave him alone. He will soon be hungry. Why don't you come here and read me the news."

His eyes were failing and he found the newspapers a strain, so he recruited her as his reader. She read in a loud, clipped, impatient voice, which increased in volume and speed as the minutes wore on. He listened patiently and she read doggedly, dutifully, although she found this chore above all others odious and horribly boring. She never told him of her dislike, but he knew it. She never told him that she cringed when he mentioned newspapers. But he knew, and he let her read never-theless.

He taught her two English phrases when he sent her to visit their eldest son in the United States. She could say "Shut up!" and "Hurry up!" and used these expressions on all occasions. They worked remarkably well as self-defense. Most people shied away from her when she spoke, and she was safe, hidden from the world.

During the war she became his master; she watched all his movements and treated him as a child, feeding him carefully according to a special schedule. All her children were gone and she had no others to care for. He was stubborn, but he sub-mitted to her will, knowing it would give her contentment and a mission to be accomplished. But his mind was set in stub-bornness, and after meals he always tried to do as he pleased. She screamed at him bitterly when he tried to walk out the door. Fearing the worst for him, in his absence she gave way to hysterical anxiety. She could never harness his stubborn inde-pendence and pride. Hadn't he gone his own way for the past eighty years?

When he was younger he bought a patch of land on the outskirts of Beirut. Although everybody told him to sell it, he clung to it tenaciously, just because he didn't like being told what to do. He would go his own way no matter what—perhaps he'd even die without selling it, perhaps he'd take the property deeds to his grave. They all panicked at the thought. Eventu-ally Beirut expanded and his patch of land became the center of the new commercial district. When the price was right he finally sold.

"The crazy old man. He was just lucky!" they said. "He knows nothing of the world and of business."

How was it possible for him to make a small fortune?

"The lucky bastard."

He sat with his books and the money fell into his lap.

"The silent trickster, the clever fool."

Scorn and resentment heaped on him behind his back, for no self-seeking businessman can stand a scholar who has made a million in spite of himself.

When he was older, when his children married and produced children, he was named Jiddo, as all grandfathers are named in the Middle East. *His grandchildren remember him as Jiddo, a gentleman, a scholar, a storyteller.*

He seemed to understand and forgive the weaknesses in human nature. His brother borrowed two hundred gold pounds from him to start a construction business, and when the business succeeded he never paid Jiddo back. He denied that the loan had ever been made. Even in the days when Jiddo had no money his brother did not pay him back; and Jiddo could not beg or grovel. He could not plead. He probably did not even know how to ask for anything. "The crazy old man. The clever fool."

Perhaps Jiddo was a fool and perhaps he was a wise man. Probably a bit of both, for wise men often achieve their wisdom through false starts and mistakes.

When Jiddo died, he died a wise man, in his own bed, with old friends and relatives, old memories near at hand. He was well acquainted with his territory. His land was an old friend with endless stories to tell.

He told stories, serious tales with morals designed to teach his grandchildren and to amuse them. Some of the words were morals cleverly disguised as jokes. He sat in a chair overlooking the balcony, and his hands, steady and methodical, dictated his pace. He never spoke in haste.

"One cold afternoon I was walking through the tundra . . . I walked for miles in the bitter wind and stopped suddenly when I came upon a little bird half-dead in the snow . . . And do you know what I did with the little bird?"

"Yes, Jiddo," his granddaughter Jumana exclaimed excitedly, impatiently, for she loved to hear him speak. She wanted him to continue the story. "Yes, Jiddo. You picked him up and put him in your thick wool jacket so that he would be warm."

"And you gave him food so that he would feel better," interrupted her brother.

Jumana glared at him and urged Jiddo to speak. "Tell us the rest of the story. Finish the story, please! We forgot the ending!"

"Well . . . I carried the cold bird in my jacket for many miles and finally he felt much better. He began to ruffle his feathers and sing. I realized I couldn't walk forever with this bird in my jacket, so I had to find a place to put him. And where do you think I put him?"

"I know where you put him. I know where!" laughed Jumana.

"I know better than her!" yelled her brother Walid.

"You put him in a big pile of yak dung!" the two children screamed with delight.

"Yes. And do you know *why* I put him there?"

"Because it would keep him warm."

"But wouldn't he smell terrible?" asked Walid, giggling at the thought.

"Yes," said Jiddo, "he would smell terrible, but I thought he would be happy there. And there was no one in the tundra to smell him. I left him in the yak dung singing happily. He sang and sang as I walked away, but a polar bear heard his pretty voice and came and ate him up."

"Why couldn't you save him?" wailed Walid.

Jumana looked at him scornfully. "Because Jiddo was already miles away from the bird when he looked back and saw the polar bear."

"Do you know what I learned from this story?" Jiddo asked.

The children were silent, for this was his line.

"I learned three things. The first is: He who puts you in it is not necessarily your enemy."

Jumana smiled but Walid looked a bit bewildered.

"The second is: He who takes you out of it is not necessarily your friend."

Walid still looked bewildered, and Jumana explained with an air of superiority: "Because Jiddo was the bird's friend and he put him into the yak dung. And the polar bear was the bird's enemy and took him out of the yak dung."

Jumana had a decidedly sensible air about her; she could interpret everything for her younger brother.

"And the third moral is: If you're in it up to your neck, keep your mouth shut."

Walid understood this one, at least on one level. He shrieked with laughter: "If the bird opened his mouth it would be full of yak dung. That would taste awful!"

Jiddo nodded and smiled, acknowledging their appreciation for his story. He was their hero, their entertainment; he replaced the stars of television and films and the heroes of sports and the Wild West.

Jumana told Jiddo that she did not care to go to America with her family. She had a pet hen, a prized gift from her great aunt Nadine, who owned a small chicken farm in the mountains. She left and Nadine took the hen, promising to care for her. Jumana returned the next summer and was taken to see her pet hen. When reintroduced she was greeted with a ribald crow.

"But she wasn't a rooster!" wailed Jumana.

Nadine looked at her in bewilderment and shrugged her shoulders in resignation.

"Are you sure?"

"You killed her! You *ate* her. I hate you!"

That evening Jiddo took her aside and told her a story.

"A very tired man walked through the hills. He was miserable and very hungry. He walked all the way from Damascus with a box full of very delicious cookies for his mother, who lived in our village. But on the road he was robbed. And who do you think robbed him?"

"Nadine did. Nadine's a witch. I hate her!"

Jiddo shook his head, "No you don't. Nadine certainly didn't rob him. A desperate man robbed him. Nadine gave him a roast chicken and he was grateful. The chicken was glad to fill the stomach of a starving man."

Nadine shuffled into dinner in her bedroom slippers, peering at everyone anxiously. Jumana glared at her. They ate in silence.

The family rested in the mountains every summer in a huge house with high ceilings. The rooms opened onto a central living room with the echo of a cathedral. Jiddo took long walks in the mountains. He delighted in them, his persistent habit, and he started on the first day of summer by climbing up the village steps. He had done this all his life.

His wife, Marie, screamed at him as he walked up the steps: "You forgot your sweater!"

"Remember—only an hour!"

"Don't climb all the steps. They will harm you!"

She was pale with anxiety. Angry eyes watching with hands on hips until he disappeared from view. When she could no longer see him, he took his jacket off, put his watch in his pocket, and walked gleefully in the middle of the road.

"I walked this road with the mules and donkeys before cars were made."

He continued to pace the road, and all passing cars granted him right-of-way. He knew these roads as no one else did. He knew of their very birth.

"The crazy old man. The silly old fool."

Jumana and Jiddo walked down the old roads at a methodical pace, passing bits of history as he pointed:

"This is the house in which I was born."

Jiddo liked Jumana to walk three steps behind him, but she always rebelled and ran ahead. It annoyed him but he grew used to her ways. She ran past a gnarled bush. Jiddo commanded her to stop and study it:

"The oldest tree in the mountains."

And then, "The oldest road."

The ancient shopkeepers. He knew them all.

Jiddo and Jumana trudged in silence.

"I am glad to walk with you. You are skinny. Skinny people walk well," said Jiddo.

"Is that why Teta Marie stays at home?" asked Jumana.

He thought of his wife and felt the watch bulging in his pocket. How many hours had he been away? She would be pacing the front walk, tense, fierce, waiting for him. Lunch would be laid neatly on the table—his yoghurt, his meat, his fruit—just as it had been yesterday. Even the maid was a tyrant in her own right. He felt besieged and thought of Kamal, his weakest brother.

Kamal once had a vegetable garden inhabited by crows. He built a flimsy scarecrow, but the invaders were not intimidated. Acknowledging his defeat, he sat in the garden all weekend, in the shade of his unsuccessful scarecrow, waving a white sheet.

"But surrendering to the crows and surrendering to your wife are very different matters," thought Jiddo.

The watch felt heavy in his pocket and he walked on briskly, intending to visit his eldest sister, Sophie. Poor Sophie.

"Your great-aunt Sophie wanted to go to school but she never could."

"Why?"

"Her father took her to the school in the neighboring village and a man in a donkey cart passed them on the road. The next day she was very sick and her father insisted that the man in the donkey cart had cast the evil eye on her. She recovered from her illness but was never allowed to go to school. That neighboring village was probably infected, cursed by evil eyes."

Jiddo smiled at the thought of such superstitions. He was a reasonable man. And it was a shame that Sophie couldn't read. Reading was his great distraction.

The last time Jumana saw Jiddo she was safe in the Lebanese mountains. The war was starting and she hid in the house, safe from everything, safe from excitement.

On the balcony they could hear the bombs and they listened to the BBC World Service. The view from the balcony and the radio narration gave them the illusion of live news. They felt they witnessed the events from a distance, news coverage with an authentic backdrop.

When a Boeing 747 was hijacked they could see the airport gleaming between the pillars of the stone balcony. They could follow the lighted runway and watch the plane landing cautiously in the distance. This event caused great excitement, and they studied it for hours, fascinated, horrified. Jumana was sleeping when the Boeing landed. Her uncle tried to drag her out of bed. Jiddo said, "Let her sleep. Why should she worry?"

Jumana, half awake, gratefully acknowledged his words. She turned her pillow over and plugged her ears. The thought of an airport peopled with hostages frightened her.

"Leave me alone. I'm so tired, why did you wake me up? I don't care."

She could not sleep, though, and a few minutes later she crept out of bed and onto the balcony to join her extended family as they listened to the "BBC World Report" and stared in disbelief at the jet in the distance. The jet was still and awkward on the vast field, like an elephant brought to rest in the wrong climate. The nose of the plane seemed to droop, as if it were bewildered by its sudden landing, and Jumana pitied it, pitied its terror and its ignorance. After all, it was only a lumbering elephant and couldn't be expected to understand.

Jiddo looked down at Beirut with tears in his eyes. This crime was too great for him. The huge jet was an invader, a monster, an unwanted omen. He knew that it was a signal of distress. He did not speak that night but sat, deep in thought, almost asleep. When his sons tried to believe that the war would end with the next cease-fire, he smiled and pretended to agree. But he knew that this war would last until the roots of the ancient quarrel were eradicated. He knew all this and he cringed at the knowledge. This scene made him feel helpless and old. He sat and listened to the BBC, speechless, aware of his own useless-ness. His regrets would not change the course of events. The news would always be the same, with or without him. Oh, he felt so tired, so sick of all this fuss. He wanted to wash his face, remove his false teeth, and crawl into bed.

"I am pitiful," he mumbled under his breath. "An old man with nothing to do."

Jumana sat next to him, saying nothing. Three days later she was driven to the airport with an army escort to protect her on the dangerous roads. *She would never forget the nausea, the terror, and, above all, the sadness, the knowledge that she would never return to this same place, that the country would change and she would not see it again until it was almost unrecog-nizable.*

Five checkpoints at the airport and she was on her plane.

In New York the next summer she received a letter from her uncle, mailed from Jordan, one month old:

"He died peacefully, in his sleep. Perhaps it is best that way."

He was buried in his village, in the family mausoleum built by his rich brother. They say the villagers laugh whenever they pass this tomb, for it is a hideous construction, a great gray mammoth on a somber and dignified hill, designed by a man with much money and little sense.

A few weeks later all her relatives arrived in New York, with her bereaved grandmother.

"The war was too much for him," they said, and left it at that.

Brother: A Memoir

(Everett Lawrence Peters: September 28, 1928–November 14, 1989)

Everett, my only brother, was four years younger than I. We were never intimate, and eventually he came to despise me. His homophobia was archetypal in its venom. When I heard of his fatal heart attack in Florida, a good month after it happened, I informed the sister who phoned me that I was utterly unmoved—relieved, in fact. "There's one less bigot on planet Earth," I said.

We were born to impoverished parents, Dorothy and Sam Peters, on a farm in northern Wisconsin. In the 1930s Dad was employed by President Roosevelt's Works Progress Administration as a common laborer helping to restore country roads. He earned $40 per month. This with regular allotments of welfare peanut butter, brick cheese, flour, salt, sugar, honey, and canned Argentine beef enabled us to survive. Dad took advantage of another of Roosevelt's programs, the Home Owner's Loan Corporation, and bought a sandy forty acres of white birch, pine, and poplar trees, extending to a small lake, Mud Minnow Lake. The cost of the forty was $250, which Dad paid off slowly from his meager wages.

Everett was the third child. I was born in 1924 when my mother was barely eighteen, my father just over twenty-one. My sister Marge was born the following year. Isolated from any true friends, ignorant of birth-control devices, frightened by our poverty, once my mother found herself pregnant with Everett, she sought to abort him. She would pile my sister and me into a frayed buggy and push us for hours over rutted and stony country roads, hoping to jar the fetus loose. When this didn't work, she sought help from Aunt Kate, who lived a mile away and was regarded as a witch both mistrusted and feared by my father. Mom ignored Dad's counsel and visited Kate, who concocted raw egg mixtures spiked with paregoric, mustard, and cow's milk traced with blood. She also recommended mustard packs so hot they burned my mother's abdomen.

At Everett's birth things went badly. Since the regular family doctor, Barney Oldfield, was unavailable, Dad returned from the five-mile drive to Eagle River in his Model-A Ford with Dr. McMurray, an alcoholic and former World War I aviator. McMurray's local claim to fame was that each Memorial Day he dropped a wreath of poppies over Eagle River.

My mother's labor was difficult. My sister and I sat at the round oak kitchen table, frightened by the screams issuing from the bedroom a few steps away. My dad, worried, kept entering and leaving the room, until finally McMurray told him that the baby was coming and that he should stay in the kitchen with us. He'd see to the birth. Everett did not reach the world yelling. In fact, the doctor told Dad that he really had to hit the kid "to get him going." Before leaving, McMurray dropped silver nitrate in Everett's eyes, wiped him, covered him in flannel, and placed him in bed beside Mom. We were allowed into the room for a few seconds.

My mother blamed the doctor for Everett's poor vision, maintaining that he had overdosed the eyes. "He was drunk," she reminded Dad. When he was five Everett wore his first pair of welfare glasses. The white of his right eye appeared filmy and strange. He seemed to have little vision there at all, and the glasses did little. Not surprisingly, he was slow to read. Before I was four, I had taught myself to read the first-year primers used in our one-room country school. Margie read when she was five. We assumed Everett was "slow," even slightly retarded. He showed no interest in books and would slam them away when we tried to read to him. Only Mom was able to keep his interest. He loved playing with empty sewing thread spools, which Dad fashioned into crude cars that rolled and spun. As I recall, Everett never had any pets. He was our wounded bird; my parents never expected as much from him in school as from us. Dad, himself uneducated beyond two years in a North Dakota prairie school, extolled education to me as a way of avoiding common labor when I was grown. Everett, he assumed, would have to accept his lot as a worker. Out of guilt for not having wanted him, Mom later confessed that she willingly spent far more hours trying to teach him than she had with us.

One fall morning when Everett was six Dad took me aside and told me that they were going to town to get the "end of Everett's peter cut off." "Why?" I asked, horrified. "He can't pee. The end's grown shut." When Everett returned that afternoon, I saw the bandages and was told that he would be sleeping with Mom until he healed—he and I had shared the same bed. For nearly a month my mother assisted him to the outhouse and sat by him, tending the bandages, helping him to urinate. Eventually, he showed me his penis. Scar tissue had formed, and the shaft looked red and sore. This was the first circumcised penis I had ever seen.

About this time, too, Everett manifested symptoms of petit mal. The attacks were twice a week and generally brief. His eyes would roll back in his head, and his lids would flicker. On occasion he would fall to the ground or to the floor, as he did once when he was chasing my next sister, Nell, born three years after Everett, around the corner of the house. In his falling, he struck his head on a rock, broke his glasses, and bled. Mom brought him round by throwing water in his face. His epilepsy disappeared shortly after he reached puberty.

Other boys at school, hearing of his difficulties, related it to his generally manic physical energy, more evidence to them of "craziness." The game he particularly loved was a wild form of tag, "pump pump pull away," which allowed him to race around the white clapboard school fast enough to catch the other students who had set out in the opposite direction. He was exercised when he felt someone was not playing fair, and would pull tantrums. He seemed to have no hobbies. When we found a nest of pink baby field mice in the deep grass of the school yard, he walked off by himself, leaving us to explore them. We finally tossed them to a tortoiseshell cat living at the school. Later, in high school, where Margie and I joined the band and entered oration and declamation contests, he lingered on in the lower grades, increasingly disaffected with reading and arithmetic. One teacher pitied him and promoted him to the seventh grade, trying to synchronize him with others his age. He towered above the other kids.

Nor was he interested in hunting and fishing, both activities Dad loved and spent much time at as a way of supplying us with fish and venison. Dad was also an excellent mechanic and would buy some old jalopy for next to nothing and within a week or so have it running. His efforts to interest Everett here also failed. Even when he gave Everett an old Model-T Ford, he did the maintenance. Everett did love fieldwork and was always proud that his rows of potatoes and beans were far straighter than ours. He was immaculate in hilling squash and corn, and seemed to love harvesting vegetables. He was too impatient, though, to pick wild blueberries and raspberries, staples for our winter diet, which Mom would can in sugar syrup and store in the root cellar. The latter you entered by pulling up a trapdoor in the living room, climbing down a wooden ladder into a sizable storage space of dank, dark earth, spiders, occasional toads, and rats.

Everett never displayed any overt jealousy over my successes at school, where I was usually the teacher's favorite. Perhaps jealousy was not in his fiber, some quirk in his brain had short-circuited that particular emotion. In our daily play, Margie and I, since we were the oldest, were generally together. Everett paired with Nell. I later discovered that he was sadistic to this younger sister. Nell reports that he would concoct horrid mixtures of green leaves and rancid water, let them ferment, then force Nell to drink. He made her eat earthworms, on penalty of taking her into the woods and killing her. She also had to drink gasoline. If she were to tell, he said, he would surely kill her—and she believed him. She did defy his sexual advances.

His sadism toward Nell possibly reflected some powerful internal rage—I simply don't know. Paradoxically, I never saw him torture an animal. When he inserted a hollow grass stem up a green frog's anus and inflated the animal, he was merely doing what other boys did. When others worried a dog or a cat, he merely stood by without participating.

What he lacked, it appears now, was a sense of decorum or appropriateness. I mean, a curious absence of moral sense (he was neither moral nor immoral, rather amoral) prevailed with him. On rare occasions when the Botteron family, with children our ages, visited, Norman Botteron, aged fifteen, would say to the rest of us: "See Everett. He can jump off the roof of the house." Everett would rush (boosted by Norman) to climb on the house, to the apex of the hip roof, where he would wait until he was sure all of us were watching and then leap down. Miraculously, he never injured himself. Everett had grown amazingly that summer, and although he was only thirteen, was nearly six feet tall. He was brawny and slender, with a sheaf of auburn hair which fell in a cowlick over his forehead. He had a craggy look, with prominent jaws and huge hands. As for his roof leapings, he had no apparent sense whatever that Norman was ridiculing him.

Later, when Dad gave him a marshy lot near the family house (we were living closer to town then), Everett proceeded to take out four separate mortgages on the same nearly useless land, seeing nothing at all wrong in keeping the news from his various lenders. Eventually, faced with suits for larceny, he left northern Wisconsin, to return thirty-five years later, just before my mother's death.

I can't remember that we ever fought. Being four years older, my sexual urges were more advanced than his, and I would attempt to engage him in boy play. He was usually resistant and would huddle under the heavy quilt my mother had made from assorted scraps of corduroy cloth, pulling the sheet up around his neck. "Don't be dirty," he'd say. "Read your Bible." I was at the time a Bible enthusiast and was superintendent of the Christ Evangelical Lutheran Sunday School. I was so devout that I would walk the eight-mile round trip to town and back almost every Sunday. My quiet aim was to read all of the Bible through, including all the "begats," then start all over again. I hoped to become a Lutheran minister. Occasionally, Everett would join me in the Lord's Prayer before falling to sleep. Mornings were always when I would try to generate sex play. When he did oblige, he would proceed immediately downstairs to report that "Bob was playing dirty." I would vehemently deny it. My parents didn't seem to care and never reprimanded me. Eventually I preferred the freedom of not having to lie when he accused me at the breakfast table. I insisted then on having my own bed.

When I reached eighteen and was drafted into the army, our lives diverged. My family spent most of the war years in Green Bay, Wisconsin, where Dad worked as a welder in the ship-yards, as part of the war effort. He later died of emphysema and cancer, brought on, he believed, by breathing galvanized fumes there. Everett also lived in Green Bay and held a series of menial jobs, waiting, so he said, until he was old enough to join the service. When they were still back on the farm, he quit school without completing eighth grade, using the excuse that he was needed to help the folks; my being drafted into the army had left them shorthanded. He had been doing wretchedly in classes, was in danger of failing, and though he was only fifteen, vowed never to step through a classroom doorway again. My parents acquiesced. The school authorities were indifferent.

After being demobilized from the army in the spring of 1946, I spent the summer at home (my family had now returned from Green Bay), preparing myself to attend the University of Wisconsin that fall. I spent much of the money I had saved during my three years in the army, via savings bonds, on a down payment for a house in town for my mother, where, for the first time, she would have running water and electricity. Everett had enlisted in the army and was in California. He loved bullish manual labor and spent his enlistment as a private, working, as I recall, for a supply unit requiring physical effort on a grand scale.

The only time we met during this period was in 1954 when, married and with a first child, I was teaching in Boston. Everett's visit was cheerful, and I was struck by his caring attentiveness to my son, Rob. He was in excellent physical shape and said he planned to make a career out of the service. Within months he was back living with my parents in Eagle River, in a shack he had built with Dad's help from scrap lumber just a few steps from Dad's welding shop. To reach Everett's you walked on planking, the marsh was so wet.

He shortly married a woman his age, who, apart from a bad complexion (Mom's theory was that she didn't use soap and water enough), was not unattractive. She wore platform wedgies, tight skirts halfway to her thigh, and blouses that set off her ample breasts. She was slim and fancied herself a talented pop singer—all she needed was a band and a chance. To keep Gladys in clothes and jewelry, Everett worked two full-time, forty-hour-per-week jobs, both of them menial—one as a janitor, the other as a gofer in a lumber company. Even when their son was born, Gladys managed her freedom well. With Everett away, she was not idle. He returned unexpectedly one evening to find the worst of the town drunks in bed with her. In the ensuing scene she berated Everett, demeaning him by announcing that she had been selling her ass all over town, and why shouldn't she, he was no damn good as a lover. She was saving her earnings to go to Chicago or Milwaukee and join a band. Moreover, the kid was not his.

Everett, devastated, sued for divorce. His lawyer was so inept that Gladys, through a better lawyer, managed to pass as the injured party, received the divorce, and had full rights to the child, convincing the judge that Everett was unfit to have anything to do with the boy. During this nightmare I let my brother down, for when he asked me to go with him to see his lawyer, I refused, saying it was better that he himself go, on a one-to-one basis. Never that I can recall had he asked me for help. I should have gone; literate in ways he was not, I might have convinced the lawyer to protect him from his wife.

He drifted through towns in various midwestern states and three years later returned home with a new woman, actually with two women, Katie and her younger sister, June, and an adolescent brother. June was barely twelve. Almost on purpose, to get even with women for Gladys's having victimized him, he found a creature so backward that she literally could not tell time, nor could she cook. He reputedly had rescued her in the midst of a vicious beating by her abusive father. He would belittle Katie in front of my parents. "Look at her, Ma," he'd laugh and point. "She can't tell time." Katie fawned over him like a subservient dog. My parents believed that Everett was sleeping with both Katie and June, and possibly even with her brother.

Over the years he had kept in touch with my oldest sister, who shared his homophobia, and who believes today, apparently, that you can get AIDS simply by being in the same room with someone who has it. He moved to Florida, became a religious fundamentalist, supported himself by small-time contracting, and lived with yet another woman, with whom he had a daughter, Dorothy. In the mid-1960s, unable to care for "Little Dorothy" properly, he sent her to Wisconsin to live with my mother, after whom the girl was named. Apparently his life was again on the skids. At one point he invited a troubled nephew to visit him and work. The youth, himself in difficulties with the law over drugs, stayed only briefly. His mother believed that Everett had put the make on him.

I saw Everett again during the week my mother died, in the summer of 1971. I was scheduled to read my poetry at the Wisconsin State University campus in Stevens Point, about two hours south of Eagle River, and it seemed a good idea for a reunion of all the kids (my father had died in 1965). My mother's clogged aorta (she'd had an operation to clear the left side, but found recuperation so foul she refused to clear the other) meant that she would not live long. She was also a chain smoker and lived on a wretched diet of sugar and fat, her favorite food being jelly rolls and doughnuts. Everett drove Mom and Nell to the Rhinelander airport to meet my plane. He was a fairly handsome, tanned, late-middle-aged man, over six feet tall, who sidled rather than walked straight on, and who loved making proclamations. Self-absorbed, he asked me nothing personal and left my sister and me to negotiate my feeble mother to the car.

The next day I spent taking down and cleaning the ceiling tiles in my mother's small house, something she asked specifically that we do because she was unable to do the job herself. Years of cigarette smoke had darkened them. Everett sat stretched out on a sofa pontificating about Florida weather, his construction jobs, niggers, and Jews. When I asked him to give me a hand, he refused, saying I always liked doing "house work." Both his voice and what he said were irritating. When

I criticized his prejudices, he grew even more assertive. I observed that he'd feel right at home wearing a KKK sheet. He said he'd joined but didn't go very often to their meetings and demonstrations. Anyway, he boasted, they'd stopped lynching niggers, which took the fun out of it. Paradoxically, he liked hiring poor Blacks, for they would work for next to nothing and do exactly what he said. He found my liberal notions thoroughly screwed. After an hour or so, I stopped talking to him.

The following morning a nephew, Marty Pietila, drove me to Stevens Point, where I was to perform and stay for two days. Marty had already returned to Eagle River when the phone call came that Mom had died suddenly of a stroke while she was sitting in a recliner chair drinking her morning coffee and watching TV. Louie Crew, the professor sponsoring me at Point, immediately drove me north, where I found that my sisters had already made funeral arrangements. I was in charge of my mother's will. Everett lingered on the periphery, giving useless advice, seemingly little touched by the event. He was anxious for the funeral to conclude so that he could return to Florida.

Before the rites, my oldest sister told Everett what he had already suspected, that I was a homosexual. When he realized that I was indeed gay (he never told me this directly—I heard about it later from my sisters), he spent the last two days of his visit incommunicado at my oldest sister's house. Back in Florida, he phoned my favorite sister, informing her that so far as he was concerned I was "dead," that he had no brother. Furthermore, she would have to choose between him or me— she couldn't be his friend if she liked me. I easily accepted his dismissal and thought no more about him until my sister Nell phoned with news of his death in Florida. He had a massive heart attack while he was laying carpet in the fundamentalist church to which he belonged. He was already dead and buried—no one knew there were relatives until a former wife going through his effects found an address book with my sister Marge's phone number.

Why do I write of him? Am I as unperplexed and unmoved by his death as I thought I was? In his mind, had I preceded him in death, as a homosexual who didn't deserve life? After nearly a year, I continue to sort out feelings. Certainly, two brothers, no matter how different, share a symbiosis of parentage, capillaries, and personal history, including massive hates. I see him now as more of a victim than I earlier realized. Was I guilty of the tabloid thinking that I found so odious in his bigotries? Part of me, no matter how I might wish otherwise, lies with him in Florida clay, and as my own death hour nears (I turn sixty-six next month), we are more kin than ever.

Richard Hoffman

Pennsylvania Power & Light

"It all depends how deep your brothers are buried," my father said. We were sitting at the kitchen table and he was taking papers from a gray steel box, removing fat, red rubber bands, sorting things into piles. "Somewhere I have a deed. The Sacred Heart allows double burial, at least that's what old Mary Becker told me years ago. But you have to go down seven feet with the first one. Where's my glasses? Here. No, that's not it. We'll have to see how deep your brothers Mike and Bob are buried."

Aunt Kitty, my father's sister, came into the kitchen and went to the windowsill over the sink where we kept my mother's medication. "You two ought to get some rest. I'm all right with her for now." She was holding the vial of pills in one hand and adjusting her glasses with the other, peering at the label. "Dare she have another one of these so soon, I wonder?"

"Give it to her if she wants one," my father said. "It don't make no difference now. Here," he said to me, sliding the metal box across the table, "see if you can find anything from the Becker Funeral Home or the Sacred Heart Cemetery."

"Wait," I said to my aunt. She was filling a glass with water at the sink. "She can't take them like that. You have to crush them in sherbet."

"Shit!" My father slammed the freezer door and reached for his wallet. "Quick!" he said, handing me a wad of bills. "Run up to the corner and get some more sherbet." I took the money from him, saw it was about thirty dollars, and peeled off three singles. "This is enough," I said. He was already walking away;

he waved his hand. "Who gives a shit. Buy ten. Buy twenty. It'll just go to the fuckin' doctors anyway."

Aunt Kitty touched me on the back of the neck so I would know to say nothing. Dad went into the living room where he'd built a smaller room in the front by the window for my mother; like the one we'd built years earlier for my brothers, it was made of two-by-fours and cheap paneling. There was a shower curtain over the narrow doorway. I saw him go in. I heard him say, quietly, "How're you feeling, sweetheart?"

That small room where my mother died is, of course, gone now. The rented hospital bed faced the large front window; hanging plants obstructed the view of the street outside. The top of the window is leaded and stained glass, deep purples alternating with tulips of opaque swirled cream and frosted panels. Heavy drapes, closed at sunset, were opened each morning at the first rumor of dawn. Generally, during her last weeks, my mother slept little, and then only in the morning when she had seen the window brighten again. Her bed was placed along one of the makeshift walls so that one of the two-by-fours served as a narrow shelf beside her for a box of tissues, her inhaler, a jar of Vaseline. Next to the gurgling oxygen compressor, her night table held her alarm clock and two pictures of her infant grandson Robert, my son.

It is a mere accident of time that my mother began to die so soon after her first grandchild was born, but the irony of it produced such pain that it sometimes seemed to me that all of nature had conspired to torture us. During her last days, among the things my mother whispered to no one in particular was, "Not now. Oh please, not now."

I left to buy the sherbet, using the back door so I wouldn't disturb my parents. I could hear my mother crying, my father soothing her, my mother saying something in a hoarse whisper. By then I had learned not to intrude.

At the funeral parlor, Dad was dissatisfied. "She never stuck out her jaw like that. That's not right." He wanted me to share, again, in his outrage.

"It doesn't matter, Dad. This isn't Mom. Mom's gone."

He sighed through his nose and gave me a look both disappointed and angry.

I was wrong.

I went forth from my mother's body and, the eldest son, I had traveled far from her. My father disciplined himself, as husband and father, lover, to come back to her body, always, back to the body of his love. His grimace was a measure of the gulf between us.

"Dolly," he said, touching her hands. He shook his head and wept.

And I understood my mother's death was not our common loss.

My mother was in the hospital two days before my father could bring himself to say the word *cancer*. "But they don't have all the tests yet."

"How's she doing? How's she feeling?"

"Jesus Christ, you know what your mother says to me? I ask her does she want anything from home and she tells me a carton of cigarettes! Fuckin' cigarettes!"

He was angry. He already knew she was leaving him.

For a time after my mother's death, I hated old women who smoked. I wanted to scream at them, "How dare you smoke and get away with it and grow old enough to tint your hair blue and be a grandmother to someone who will grow up to remember you?"

Robert likes to look through the album of our wedding pictures. He used to ask, "Who that lady?"

"That's your grandma who died. You don't remember her, but she loved you very much."

"Why she die?"

"She was very sick."

"Why?"

Later, he would point to her in the picture and call her "my grandma who died."

"That's right."

"I want to see her."

"Well, there she is. In the picture."

"But why I can't see her?"

One morning, when Robert was small enough to hold in the crook of my arm, my lips against his silky head, I dozed and dreamed that he and I were at an outdoor celebration. There was a big yellow-and-white-striped tent like the one Kathi and I had at our wedding. I was holding Robert proudly. People bent to him and touched and patted me, nodding and smiling. We were seated at a very long table, across from a radiant old man. I asked him why we were celebrating, and he said there was no occasion, that he and all the others were always there, didn't I know that? I suddenly felt that I did. I propped Robert in his little plastic seat on the table. "We're always here; we're family," the old man said, touching Robert and smiling at me.

The food was delicious. The baked beans were my mother's. She used to make them for picnics when I was a boy. I wanted more. The food was under the yellow-and-white-striped tent. I heaped the plate high and ate some right away, on my way back to the table.

They were gone, all of them. Robert's yellow seat was on the table, empty. Oh no. Oh no no no no no. Again I felt that I knew what had happened. I saw the old man in the distance, walking away. "Wait!" I called, and ran to catch up to him.

He turned and said, coldly, what I fully expected to hear. "You didn't take care of him so he's been taken from you." I tried to grab the old man, but I fell, helpless, and lay on the ground.

I woke, and Robert stirred in the hollow underneath my chin but remained asleep, his tiny mouth making sucking movements. He had given me the dream as a gift: without the small warmth of him to wake to, reassured, I would never have let myself have that dream. I would never have been able to feel, if only briefly, the horror and despair and shame of losing him. For the first time I touched, for merely a dreaming moment, the kind of pain my parents must have felt, grieving for my brothers.

When I was little I went to the beauty salon with my mother and grandmother. I was alone; that is, Bobby was not along. The salon was the front of someone's house; we went into the kitchen, where I was given cookies and milk while the women had coffee. After some talking, Mammy Etta told my mother to go first, and Mom got up and followed the other woman to the front room and they closed the door. I was scared. Horrendous noises came from behind the door: sputtering water, various motors, and one that went on a long time and sounded like a power saw. I screamed and cried. The woman came to the door—the woman, not my mother. When she opened the door I was hit by a vile stench. I was sure that the woman was a devil who was doing something awful, painful, perhaps sexual, to my mother. I threw my glass at her and screamed; when my grandmother reached to pick me up I kicked her. She shook me and said, "Your Mommy can't come out now. Stop it! Bad boy. Do you want a spanking?" I shut up, but I was sure that my mother was hurt or she would have come to me. The smell was hanging in the air so thick I puked. After a while my mother came to me and picked me up and took me outside, where we tore up bread together to throw to the birds. She had had a "permanent."

My mother's hair was always lacquered, blacker than it was when she was young. Once she was embarrassed when I came home from college a couple of days early and she hadn't gotten to the salon and I saw her roots. She said her roots were showing. Shame, that goes to the roots: my mother bore two congenitally ill, doomed sons. For her, muscular dystrophy was a mythic curse: only males are afflicted by it, and only females carry it. A genetic defect. I can imagine my mother washing her face in the morning, looking at herself in the mirror, protecting herself, vigilant against the gray or silk-white roots that prove the past, that say that time is once, once, once. For so many years she knew her sons would die before her that she had to deny time every day to be there for them, to feed them, wash them, bring them books, papers, and pencils, change the channel, bring the pisspot. Michael screamed in the night most every night for five or six years, waking everyone. She slept in a chair downstairs so she could wake him faster from his nightmares. How could she possibly believe one life is all there is? She insisted we'd be together again. She seldom went to church. She went to the cemetery, often. She had kept them alive inside her once before. "We'll be together again someday," she always said.

Mike, then Mammy Etta, then Bob: my mother lost her mother and two sons within a two-year span. She was careful to hide her bitterness; she went deep inside herself and stayed there, at the same time constructing some other person to present to us. This "person" was cheerful, busy, brimming with jokes, gossip, idle chatter. It was as if she herself were absent but had created some rough replica of herself through which she attempted to go on with her life. I pretended not to see this, played along with it; we all did. She'd tell the same jokes over and over, sometimes within the same conversation. She'd talk about the rising price of peas or lettuce, and if the conversation lagged, she'd mention it again, sometimes in exactly the same words. Her jokes were painfully self-conscious, as if she were trying to demonstrate that she was the same old fun-loving Mom.

She was only going through the motions. "I bought the roast because it was on sale. I'd planned on making pork chops but they were awfully high—last week they were two eighty-nine and now they're up to three forty-nine, it's just ridiculous . . . Oh, Marietta told me a good one last week—this guy goes into a bar and . . . I'm going to put some onions in with the roast, you always liked that . . . I can't believe it what they're getting for pork chops . . ."

Occasionally, however, Mom would hint at what was really going on inside her, but always in such a way that further conversation about it was impossible. Sometimes she talked about Henry, the grocer in our old neighborhood who'd committed suicide. She mentioned this many times and always asked if I remembered him. Of course. He and my mother had a secret that intrigued and mystified me when I was a kid. I often went to the store for my mother after school, before I was allowed to go out and play. Sometimes my mother instructed me to see Henry, no one else; I was to ask for "a box of jiggers." There was something mysterious, perhaps forbidden, going on. When I asked Henry about it he said, "Never you mind," in a way that made my imagination flare and strain to think what they could be. He had to get them down from the highest shelf with a calipers on a long stick; it was a light blue box with a pink rose on it. By the second grade I could read enough to sound out the words and sometimes guess at the meanings. I knew what a napkin was, and sanitary meant something about dirt or toilets, I wasn't sure. I had to know. I got my candy money by collecting empty bottles around the neighborhood, two cents for the small ones and five cents for the big ones, and when I had enough I went to see Henry. I ran two blocks to a lot behind the Presbyterian church and tore open the box. They were white, with cotton squares like the bottom of jewelry boxes, sealed with a tissue like kleenex, and with a little blue stripe down the middle. I thought they must be bandages. Not long after that, I found one in the garbage can, bloody, covered with flies. They *were* bandages. I had figured out the secret: *my mother was hurt, wounded, but she was too brave to tell us.*

"It's all my fault. It's all my fault," she wailed back home after Mike was buried. I took her by the chin and tried to make her look at me.

"Bullshit, Mother!" I said, a whispered scream. Relatives came over to us.

"What's the matter?" asked my uncle Bert. "Come on now, Dolly, come on," he said to her as if he were soothing a horse. She reached for him and sobbed and dried her eyes and turned to me and hugged me. "I'm okay," she said.

At last the call from the hospital came; Mom was in the recovery room. The surgeons had removed her right lung. Later we received another call informing us that she was no longer in recovery and we could see her briefly. My father grabbed his jacket, fished in his pocket for the car keys, threw them to me.

At the front door to the hospital, Dad fell behind, and I was through the automatic door before I noticed. I turned and saw him standing against a concrete post with his head down. I turned back, but the door was one-way so I had to go back out through the revolving door. When I touched his arm and asked if he was okay, he lifted his head, jaws clenched, face red and wet, and said, through his teeth, "I've spent half my life in this fuckin' hospital."

On the intensive care unit, visitors are allowed only on the hour, one at a time, for a total of ten minutes. "Oh, what kind of bullshit is this now," Dad said, grabbing the handle of the heavy door. It was locked.

"Wait," I said, "It's twenty of."

My father was leaning against the door, cupping his hands around the small window, looking in. Through the window of the other door, I could see nothing but the curtains around each bed, a nurse wearing a lab coat and carrying a small tray, one machine with tiny red lights and gauges and wires plugged into it like a switchboard.

Dad went in first. When he returned to the corridor I asked him if Mom was awake. He covered his face with his hand and nodded, and I walked past him onto the unit.

I'd forgotten to ask which bed was Mom's, and I walked down the center aisle looking to both sides. I remember seeing one patient, man or woman I couldn't tell, lying there, mouth gaping, eyes wide open. He or she could not have weighed a hundred pounds. I almost passed my mother's bed, the curtains parted to the width of a doorway. For a moment I wasn't sure it was her. Her mouth was open wide around a blue plastic hose connected to a machine at the head of her bed. *Whoosh. Click.* Her face was white and wet with perspiration, and her hair, fanned out around her on the pillow, was grayer than she'd ever let us see, only the last couple of inches still black. Her eyes were closed; when I touched her hand, they opened quickly and rolled in panic until she found me. She gripped my thumb, and I was startled and reassured by the strength in her hand. But I felt her desperation in her grip. "You made it," I said.

A week later she came home from the hospital, minus one lung, and her voice was barely audible because the surgeons had had to scrape the spreading cancer from her larynx. Tipping up her oxygen mask to speak, she held out her hand to me. "Look at my fingers," she rasped. "They're not yellow anymore. I quit."

My mother always corrected people who thought that Dolly was short for Dolores, then she'd tell a story. "When the nurse handed me to my mother, all wrapped up in a blanket, my mother bent over me and said, 'Oh you little Doll . . . eeeee!' " And she mimed shock and horror, as if the little "doll" were so ugly as to produce the shrieked second syllable of her name.

The Christmas before my mother's death, we were passing around a fresh Polaroid snapshot of the family, and as it faded into the present, my mother placed her thumb over her face and said, "Nice picture." None of us knew what to say.

When she was younger, my mother's discomfort with herself might have been mistaken for vanity. I remember her sitting at the kitchen table in a white satin robe and slippers, smoking, rolling her hair into flat curls she fastened with bobby pins. The robe had an iridescent pattern that made me think it was made of very thinly sliced wood. I'd seen that same kind of pattern on the shiny chasuble our pastor, Father Walters, wore at Mass. I must have been about four years old. I was very interested in peoples' costumes. I thought people chose to do the things they did so they could wear the costume they wanted. Firemen agreed to fight fires so they could wear firemen's hats and boots. If you were happiest in a gray denim cap and red neckerchief, the thing to do was learn to drive a train.

Sometimes I convinced myself that I was Superboy, down from Krypton, left for safekeeping in this family until I grew up and could let on who I really was. In the meantime, I was sure that my mother knew who I was but that she didn't know I knew so she never mentioned it. She wanted me to have as normal a childhood as possible under the circumstances.

I remember playing on the light green linoleum of the

kitchen floor, coloring and talking to my mother and sometimes to myself. She sat sideways at the table, leaning forward
to pluck her eyebrow with a tweezer, peering into a round mirror she held in her other hand. Sometimes her concentration
was so fierce it was hard for me to penetrate her solitude. The
mirror made things look bigger. The other end of the tweezers
had a hole in it which she pressed against her forehead, her
cheeks, her chin. It left red circles all over her face. She kept
wiping the end of the tweezers on a tissue she held in her hand
along with the mirror. It looked like she was hurting herself. A
lipstick-tipped Chesterfield burned in a heavy glass ashtray.

"But what *are* blackheads?" I asked.

"They're ugly, that's what they are." A drag on the Chesterfield. Squinting through smoke. Exasperation at the curl that
had unwound from its bobby pin. "Leave me alone now. Draw
me a nice picture or something."

My memories of these kitchen evenings are vivid, and I sus-
pect that there was a particular night of the week when my
father took my brother Bob with him and left me with my
mother and her magnifying mirror. Probably those times I remember being alone with my father, walking uptown to look
in the store windows, or walking through the cemetery with its
urns and angels, squirrels and muzzled cannons, were nights
when Bob stayed home and maybe wondered at my mother's
fierce impatience with herself. I don't know.

I remember an earthquake no one else recalls. It was a summer night, moths bothering the screen door, lightning bugs
plentiful in the yard. I was lying on the cool linoleum floor. I
have a vague memory of having done something wrong. I had
been crying, probably throwing a tantrum on the floor, when
I felt the house begin to shake. The screen door opened and
closed and a moth flew in, in just that space of time. There was
a low rumbling and trembling. My father said something about
an earthquake and went to call the Pennsylvania Power and

Light Company. My mother, in her satin robe, held me on her slippery lap. Bob may have been there too; I don't remember. No one else remembers any of this. Over the years, whenever I'd bring it up, my mother always said, "Get the hell out. An earthquake. You're dreaming."

My mother's voice, her "Dutch" accent, is hard to render on the page. The pitch and lilt of the Pennsylvania Dutch accent is, I think now, beautiful for its tone of innocent questioning, the voice generally swelling once about mid-sentence before concluding like a question even when it isn't. Not to mention the integrity of its stubbornly German syntax. I didn't always think so, however, and thinking of the years I spent as a young man trying to shed that inflected speech, I am struck by how pervasive was my mother's influence on me, not to mention the persistence of her shame. She was stuck between not wanting to talk "dutchified" and not wanting to sound "citified," which she was afraid would be construed as putting on airs.

My mother taught me to devalue her. Even that sentence— let it stand—blames her for everything, including the shame I feel for having been ashamed of her. I grew up watching which fork the others were using, what they were wearing, what they were talking about, what they seemed to be thinking. They, whoever they happened to be, had the power to find us wanting. "I'm not going to take you anywhere anymore unless you learn how to behave."

The only picture I have of my mother as a child has been, literally, defaced: she scratched out her face with something sharp and scribbled over it with a red crayon. I asked her about it once. She avoided saying why she did it. "Boy, did I get a lickin' for that," she said.

I was sitting on a kitchen chair next to her bed in the make-shift room. It was night. The only sounds in the house were the bubbling plastic cup on the oxygen compressor and the sibilance of my mother's shallow breathing. Her face changed, continually, as I watched. From time to time she mumbled something and I leaned close to her.

"I know," she said softly. "I know. I lose. But don't do this to me. Who are these people? No, I paid. Tell him I paid. I won't do that. No, not unless you show it to me first. Ah. It's beautiful."

Another time she whispered, fiercely, "No! Let go of me. Don't touch me!" And when I released her hand, her eyes opened wide and she grabbed for me in panic. "No no, not you, not you."

A coughing spasm woke her. Her grip hurt my hand. She pressed the button to raise herself in the bed, plucked at pink tissues in a box beside her, and coughed. She let go of my hand a moment and with a frantic gesture let me know that I should switch the green plastic tube from the compressor to the tall tank in the corner that put out more oxygen. I started to rise, but she grasped my arm and shook her head. "Mom, I can't switch it over without getting up." Her nails dug into my wrist. She was choking. Shaking her head. Crying.

Once she asked for her mirror. "Wait till your brothers get a load of this," she said to me, staring at herself.

"Don't you have a holy candle?" Aunt Kitty asked.

"Agh," my father said. "A holy candle. How the hell should I know?"

"She should have a holy candle when she crosses." She spoke as an exasperated adult speaks to a difficult child. "It isn't right. She has to have a holy candle burning when she crosses."

"Hold on," I said. I went upstairs to my parents' bedroom, where I knew I would find two blessed candles inside the hollow mahogany crucifix above their bed. When I took it down, the plaster behind it crumbled and the nail it had hung on fell down inside the wall. I touched the cracked and yellowed ivory Jesus and then pressed upward gently until the cross slid away, tongue-in-groove, to reveal a compartment containing a vial each for holy water and holy oil, both dry now; two candles, short, wicks burnt; and a slot into which the crucifix could be placed upright. I hadn't handled it since I was a boy, when someone, maybe my mother, showed it to Bob and me; we'd been curious about it because at school we were learning about the sacraments. The one called Extreme Unction scared us. We wondered if you had to die once the priest anointed you with the holy oil. Was it too late then to get better? What if the priest was too anxious and wanted to hurry up and get someplace else? Bob and I called it the death kit. We invested it with mystery: it could keep away devils and protect you from Hell, but once you invoked its power you had to die.

I couldn't decide whether to bring the whole "kit" downstairs or just one candle. I took one candle from its cavity and began to slide the crucifix back into place; then I did a curious, reflexive thing: I held the candle to my nose and smelled it. It *was* my mother who showed this to us; I remembered her explaining to us, with her convert's zeal and awe, that only candles made of pure beeswax could be blessed by the priest and made holy. "You can always smell a real beeswax candle," she said, and after drawing one under her nose with her eyes closed, "Hmmmmmm," she held it out for Bob and me to smell. I put the candle back, slid Jesus back in place, and brought the whole cross downstairs.

I was about to get my coat. I needed to walk outside, once around the block, fresh air. Aunt Kitty waved me to her, put her hand on my arm. "Stay." I went back into the small room and knelt by the side of the bed. Dad placed my hand on Mom's leg. It was cold. Both Dad and Aunt Kitty nodded when I looked at them. I felt my mother's wrist for a pulse; for a moment I was sure I felt one, then there was none. Within moments the cold crept up her body as if death were pulling a blanket over her.

My father rested his forehead on the bed beside her, and I stroked his back and rested my hand on the back of his neck. I remember that my relief, after so long a struggle, was so great that I had a strange impulse to congratulate my mother for what she'd accomplished at last. For a moment I thought I could take her by the hand, now that her agony was over, and she would sit up and smile with triumphant fatigue. It's hard to render this feeling: as if she'd just struggled mightily to give birth, or as if we had been waiting merely for a fever to break, or as if we'd been waiting with impatience for an hourglass to run out so we could turn it over again. I remember hearing the buzz and click of the clock-radio on her nightstand then, the sound of the next minute falling into place, and for that one moment I was as shocked by her death as I would have been had she been healthy and died in an accident or inexplicably in her sleep.

On the way to the cemetery, in the gray limousine, we all stared straight ahead. The cortege moved slowly, headlights on. Although they couldn't see the dark we drove through, people waited patiently. A man on the sidewalk removed his hat.

The Death of Fred Astaire

In the summer of 1984 I lived for six weeks in Ludlow, Vermont, with my lover's cocker spaniel. I had known the lover (we'll call her Dale) and the dog (Coney) for about a year, and at this point I was fonder of the lover. Cockers were not my preferred breed, and this one was overweight and undertrained; prone to stomach, back, and ear aches; an obsessive humper; clingy and wimpy. I couldn't understand why he'd insist on sitting by the feet of a nearly motionless human tapping out the first draft of a novel when he could have been romping through the woods with the gang of more doggy dogs who lived up the road. I wasn't flattered. I felt crowded. And every time I shifted positions or sighed, his ears would perk and he would rise and wag in anticipation of an outing.

I suppose it snuck up on me slowly. I remember searching the Grand Union parking lot for the shadiest spot, and then my pleasure at seeing his delight when I returned with my bundles. I worked hard trying to teach him to eat his biscuits from the kitchen floor instead of the living room Oriental—even harder trying to teach him to stick by my heels when we ran. On the dumb side, but with a frightening desire to please, he was eminently trainable; I felt my terrible power over him and struggled to use it responsibly. However it happened (clutching his silky fur through those middle-of-the-night thunderstorms, spying his motionless form waiting on the bank as I swam to shore), three, maybe four weeks into our enforced, often irksome intimacy, I found myself planning my afternoon outings with him in mind.

To be fair, his tastes and mine were similar; nevertheless, there were days I quit work early because he had been sitting so patiently, so glumly; days I chose to go one place rather than another because I knew he would enjoy it more. And when I realized this—that I had become a person capable of making sacrifices, however minor, for a dog who wasn't mine and wasn't the kind of dog I would have chosen—and then when I realized it was no longer a question of putting his desires before mine, because his pleasure had become my own— then I knew I wanted a baby.

This wasn't exactly news. As a child, I always imagined I'd one day be a mother. And a friend recently reminded me of our first lunch in 1975, when I told her, "with great earnestness and passion," that what I most wanted was to get married and raise a family. Five years after that, sitting in the car with Karen, my first woman lover (Dale was my second), I told her that even though I loved her, had never felt more in love, never been happier in my life, I knew we wouldn't last more than a few months because I wanted to get married and have children. When Karen and I broke up two years later, I again began to search for a man to start a family with—despite the fact that when I encountered mothers with their children I had difficulty imagining myself so engaged with the tedium, so patient and loving. Only now, with Coney providing evidence (reliable or not) that I had what it takes, did my desire for children change from being a rather abstract assumption about some future I could not seem to catch up with to a yearning I could taste. This both pleased and panicked me. I was thirty-three. Dale and I were planning to live together in the fall, and this arrangement was not likely to lead to anyone's pregnancy.

I had heard of lesbians raising children together when one or both had given birth while married. I had heard of lesbians adopting children and even of conceiving them themselves through artificial insemination, but I felt sure these options were for other people: committed lesbians, women who had always known, or who didn't but once they came out realized the signs had been there all along; women who not only loved women but thought it better to love women; women who had great anger or bitterness about aspects of their own childhoods and thought raising children with women would be a better way to raise children and would result in better children, a better world, or rather, planet. I was none of these women.

Though none of my many relationships with men had lasted more than a couple of years, I considered them as happy and healthy as most I had seen. I had loved some of these men and was still attracted to men. I liked watching them play basketball, fiddle with car engines, hoist sails, dress wounds, argue in court. I had always enjoyed wearing my boyfriend's shirts—they made me feel thin and sexy; and nothing turned me on more than the sight of a man holding an infant in the crook of his arm or throwing a baby into the air.

Certainly I considered myself a feminist. I recognized ways in which I had compromised myself in my relationships with men; I had discovered that when I was with women I felt more fully myself and more deeply loved. Still, I had never been entirely comfortable with terms like "overthrowing the patriarchy," probably because in many ways that patriarchy had treated me well. I remembered my childhood as happy, had only minor complaints about the way my parents had raised me, and perhaps most significant of all, I was a daddy's girl—a fact apparently so obvious that even though I never had much of a voice, in a camp production I was the one who sang "My Heart Belongs to Daddy." As a child, I was Daddy's little helper, trotting behind him with the rake, the caulking gun, the monkey wrench. He taught me to ride a two-wheeler, to keep my head throughout a geometry proof. His loves were my loves—invigorating music, the color red, veal parmigiana, Adlai Stevenson, the first forsythia; his values my values—

naturalness, honesty, independence, persistence, daring, conversation, family. In my early twenties I began to discover the many things I admired in my mother (her graciousness, generosity, intuitive feminism, intelligence, love of art and literature—in short, her depth of feeling and understanding), but up until then, it was my father I held on high and aimed to please, and the thought that my little girl (for of course, I would have a little me) might not have a father at all, and certainly not in the same way I had mine, this was nothing I was ready to imagine.

Of course, as a child of the 1960s, I did not want to replicate my parents' lives, but my idea of doing things differently consisted of marrying a man with long hair, maybe an earring, most likely a non-Jew with an unimpressive income; of doing it not in a temple or country club but on some mountaintop, *sans* ice sculptures, *avec* wildflowers. It was preferring chamber music to symphonies, sending my children to Quaker camps, never consulting an "interior decorator." It did not include, as the title of one of the books I eventually read on the subject put it, "Having a Baby Without a Man."

Perhaps if my mother had once been a night-club singer, or my sister had eloped with a goy, or my father had been married once before—if anyone in my immediate family had had just the tiniest secret or blemish. Or if I had frequently felt left out or had to endure taunts. But we were Jews who lived among Jews, and my experience with feeling different or oppressed went no further than having been briefly forced to wear shoes with protruding metal plates designed to correct my pigeon toes, no further than occasionally being the last to be chosen for a softball team. When my sister, who was studying physical therapy, discovered that (like many people) one of my legs is slightly longer than the other, I felt truly shaken. And when I was in my first lesbian relationship—well, on the one hand, accustomed as I was to approval, I told nearly everyone and was often bold, even cavalier. On the other hand, I had dreams about being corraled and branded, I lived in dread of so much as a raised eyebrow, I daily chose to look as straight—no straighter—than I always had. And when I knew, really knew, I wanted a baby, I thought: this having-a-baby-without-a-man idea—it may be fine for lots of people, but not for me.

So why didn't I just tell Dale I couldn't move in with her? I guess because I loved her, loved the way she loved me. Because I had confidence in our ability to live together happily (a rare feeling for me). Because as much as I might lampoon those Be Here Now, Go with What You Feel folks, I knew they had something to teach ruminating planners like me. Or maybe (because I had climbed mountains, run races, written novels, gone to dark lesbian bars?) I faintly suspected I might someday be able to consider what, at present, felt beyond me (and when we first met and I casually asked Dale if she wanted children she had said yes).

What I know for sure is that I wanted a baby soon, but not immediately, and so when a visiting friend pointed out, while we picked raspberries to calm my nerves, "Just because you move in with someone doesn't mean you can't move out!"— even though I knew this was just the sort of thinking that simply traded bearable pain in the near future for agony later on—I found myself repeating the line in my head, even quoting it to friends, as if it contained some lifesaving truth.

No doubt the line was not far from my mind that late August morning I was readying the house for my departure. Coney, fearful of being left, was constantly at my heels, and "My Fair Lady" was on the radio. Though I had long ago decided show music was too lowbrow for sophisticated me, I was singing along and loving it. But then "The Rain in Spain" came on, and around the time Professor Higgins's "no-no-no" talk gave way to his "yes-by-gosh-she's-got-it" song, I noticed my throat had clamped shut. I bore with it another round or two, but soon I dropped the sponge, slumped down, and gave in to the feeling. Then, just a minute or so later, after I had wiped the tears, I was left wondering: what was that all about?

The song was a happy one, not about anything that particularly hit home, except maybe that Higgins trained Eliza in much the same stern way I trained Coney and we both fell in love, but no, I didn't think that was it. Back to my scrubbing, I was remembering how we used to sing out at the tops of our lungs—my Daddy and I—mimicking Rex's haughty Britishness and howling along with Julie's triumphant "Spaaains" and "plaaains." I was remembering his black hair and red cheeks and my throat was tightening again as I thought (not without *some* amusement): well, maybe I'm sad because it looks like I'm *not* going to marry my father after all. Nor even a man like him. Nor any man at all.

Months later, when a friend asked, "If Dale were a man would you marry her?" I quickly said, "Yes." We loved being together, had together created a beautiful home (with, come to think of it, much help from "our architect," the yuppie's interior decorator). One friend who had spent a weekend commented on the balance, the grace she saw in our lives. I was touched; I felt it, too. And Coney—he was healthier, happier, more disciplined, thinner, and, most important, equally wild about each of us.

And so, when I saw a notice about a discussion at the women's center on lesbian parenting, off I went—alone, for although Dale had said she was interested in raising children with me, she believed coming out or being found out would jeopardize her job, and unlike me who has a large appetite for hashing things out in groups, she tends to make her decisions in private.

I had expected the discussion to be geared to lesbians considering parenting; probably I had assumed it would be, like many feminist events, an upbeat, cheerleading sort of thing. What it turned out to be was a support group for women already doing it, women who clearly needed support. The children being discussed were all troubled in one way or another. One teenage daughter was so intent on proving her heterosexuality that she had become, according to her mother, a "slut." Another daughter's best friend's parents had prohibited their daughter from visiting. A boy avoided the problem by never inviting his friends home. One woman's ex-husband had threatened to sue for custody. Another woman, a "nonbiological mom," certain that no one at her job could handle her situation, lied when she needed to go home to tend her sick child. And another "coparent" (another new word for me) was tired of her lover's daughter hating her. They all seemed tired; and they all had money problems. Still, not wanting to feel daunted, I focused on how much I liked the women, how impressed I was by their strength, integrity, and resiliency. I reminded myself that in all cases, their children, born while the mother was married, had expectations of normalcy and a relatively recent relationship with the coparent. Finally, though I knew I ought not feel anything but guilt and outrage over my class privilege, I consoled myself with the observation that these women (or most of them) were not so privileged, and that perhaps I, with my sense of entitlement, not to mention my actual entitlement (a degree from an elite college, relatively wealthy and always generous parents), would be spared some of these women's difficulties.

It must have been that same winter (the first we lived together) that I attended (this time with my ex, Karen, and her new girlfriend) a local health clinic's introductory meeting on "artificial insemination," as it was called then, before they changed it to "alternative insemination," for "really, there's nothing artificial about it." I can't remember how I first heard about this meeting, but I had to call the clinic and, without mentioning my purpose, ask for a certain person. Only then was I told the time and place. I was shocked by all this secrecy. It had never occurred to me that what I was contemplating was risky in any realm other than the social or emotional. I still don't know what law I was breaking or what the clinic feared (loss of funding, bad press, chastisement from the archdiocese?), but as I entered the specified building and located the basement stairs, I felt like a novice member of some underground cadre meeting to plan their next bombing.

At this gathering, in addition to the three of us, were a straight single woman in her late thirties; a straight-looking, very-much-in-love-looking lesbian couple; a less straight-looking but also loving-looking interracial lesbian couple; and the two presenters, a nurse and a lawyer.

The nurse spoke first: The sperm was flown in from a bank in Oakland; someone met it at the airport with dry ice—even so, it was crucial that the client get to the clinic within a few hours (of course, all of this had to be carefully coordinated with one's cycle); each insemination cost fifty dollars, and usually one did two or three a cycle; on the average, pregnancy was achieved after about six months, but sometimes it took years; one's chances for a healthy pregnancy and baby were no better or worse with "AI"; the bank screened its donors carefully, but there were no guarantees—though their donors were not paid, which meant they were more likely to answer the questionnaire honestly; one received some basic information, including donor's height and weight, race and religion, hair and eye coloring, occupation, and special talents; there were two possible arrangements—either the father would stay forever unknown, though you could get certain medical information, or the father could become known when the child reached eighteen.

As for the news from the legal front: Yes, it was possible that your baby could be the half sibling of someone else's child and not know it and fall in love (heterosexual) with that person and perform incest and give birth to the kind of child born from such unions; yes, although they were very cautious in their labeling, names were never used and a mix-up wasn't impossible and you could end up with a baby who was of a different race than you had ordered; and yes, it was possible in the case of donors who never intended to identify themselves that the child could have a medical condition which necessitated genetic information beyond the basics on record and that information would be impossible to obtain; and no, she didn't know if there were copies of the records or what would happen if there was a fire in the building that housed them.

The above were answers to questions from the group, questions I would never have thought to ask. What I thought to ask but didn't was, What do I tell my child when she asks who her father is? What do I say when she is older and wants to know who I thought I was that I could choose to deprive her of a father? And will we—the child and I—spend the rest of our lives (or a mere eighteen years) walking down the street, into the supermarket, onto the airplane, searching the eyes of strangers for the man who was her father?

Such questions told me that neither the eighteen-year wait nor the life of eternal ignorance were the right routes for *me*. And artificial insemination, the actual process of racing to the clinic and climbing upon a cold metal table—well, there was nothing inherently horrible about it, unless a person had once had rather different images of conception. Which is all to say that although I dutifully took notes (for I could no longer assume that what was out of the question at the present would remain that way), when I got home I began the list in the back of my little black journal. It includes former lovers, men I had dated once or twice, old friends, husbands of friends, friends of friends, someone I once shared an office with, my car mechanic . . . I remember trying to maintain a brainstorming mentality, but I see now I must have censored from the start. Absent, for example, are the names of my one gay male friend (the HIV test wasn't out yet) and a straight man I came close to marrying—not because I felt this would be too sticky but because of his sister's colitis, his brother's asthma, his father's blood pressure. I remember thinking that if I had married him, none of this would have prevented me from wanting his child; I also remember realizing that if Dale and I could mate and I was applying the same strict standards to her family history, she would not have passed the test. Still, I told myself it was entirely appropriate that I should apply different standards to a donor than to a husband or mate, and when the word *eugenics* grazed my mind, I swallowed the bad taste and refused to be stymied.

Shortly after I entered the first round of names, I received a formal-looking envelope from someone on the list, an old college friend who had, for one night, been my lover. Though I had been sure this man wasn't for me (too intense, too wounded, too spiritual), when I saw the wedding invitation, I couldn't not, at least for a moment, think that I could have— *should* have—been the one to marry him. More lingering was the realization that his marriage would make it less likely— no, just about impossible—that he would want to father a child with me. It seemed to mock the whole plan, exposing its full ridiculousness, its inevitable failure. (I declined the invitation, never even sent a present.) And the longer I looked at my list, the clearer it became that really, there were hardly any genuine possibilities—certainly not the husbands of friends, especially not the one whose wife had just had a hysterectomy (and to think I had once viewed that as an auspicious sign!); not the ones I barely knew; or the one who had horrible teeth; or the one who would insist on the kid going to his alma mater; or the one who might interpret a missing button or dirty face as a sign of bad mothering; or the one who once he had his "own" children would forget our kid's birthday; or the one who was probably still in love with me; or the one who worked in a lab with blood; or the ones who might not be absolutely, unequivocally okay on the lesbian issue.

That didn't leave many, but in the spring of 1985, after endless discussions with Dale (another story), I wrote Jim (one of the old friends, first on the list) and asked if he'd consider fathering my child. He promptly replied with an antique postcard, a photo of an elegantly dressed man and woman in a rowboat, its title something like "Lifelong Friendship." Jim's own words were brief: "Very flattered, very nervous, very interested."

How perfect! I thought. The photo, its title, his message. For a few minutes at least, this no longer seemed like such a crazy idea.

That summer, I was further spurred on when I visited a childhood friend, a lesbian who'd recently had a baby. Carol lived with her lover, her lover's teenaged son from her married years, and Carol's four-year-old daughter, conceived by AI. When I went to dinner, I was relieved to see that the daughter was a normal, pretty little girl (I don't know what I expected), adored by her older "brother," an unusually thoughtful and articulate sixteen-year-old. What I most remember from the evening was how at bedtime the daughter climbed into her coparent's lap and clung happily to her, in no way displaying confusion over her breasts and smooth cheeks.

Though normally I'm a sucker for crisp Yuppie cafés, when my parents were visiting from New York about a year later, I suggested a large, noisy deli I hoped would make them feel at ease (despite the small portions and inferior rye bread). I'd already given my parents three blows—that I was involved with a woman, involved with a second woman, moving in with the second—still, telling them my latest plan wasn't going to be easy: it would slam the door on any lingering hope that this was all just a phase. More important, it (or the baby, anyway) would slam that same door on me. Preparing for this moment in therapy, I often cried. I certainly didn't want to cry now—nor did I want to sound overly casual about the potential problems. In my previous comings out to my parents I had struggled with similar conflicts, and while proud to have shielded them from the depth of my pain and uncertainty, I also longed for them to know the real me.

In any case, they took the news calmly. (The Bloody Marys I suggested probably helped. Also, my mother wasn't entirely surprised—she knew I'd visited Carol and that had started her wondering.) Quickly getting into the spirit of the thing, they began arguing in favor of an unknown donor. This surprised and embarrassed me. I figured they, of all people, would share my desire for a live and involved father, that link to hetero-sexuality who could provide at least a whiff of normalcy. But they were more concerned about the possibility of "compli-cations." And they were not alone. Dale had mixed feelings on the issue. My sister, her husband, and several friends with firsthand knowledge of disastrous situations involving a known father felt as my parents did. Nevertheless, I proceeded with my plans—albeit rather slowly, in part because I had my own anxieties, but also because I had started a new teaching job and didn't think it wise to get pregnant my first year, especially since I wasn't married.

About a year after our lunch at the deli and shortly after a weekend family party celebrating my father's sixty-fifth, I phoned my parents to discuss the latest baby news. I mention the celebration because it was in part responsible for my deci-sion to view my folks as potentially helpful allies in this project. We'd all gotten along well over the weekend, and my parents had been particularly warm to Dale, who, for the first time, felt fully accepted into our clan. Also, the poem I'd written for my father had been a big success; and after my recitation, as my father walked toward me with open arms, oblivious to everyone else in the room, even his beloved brother who had traveled so far to be there, I could see that even after I had betrayed him (for that's how I thought of it—he'd given me his all so that I might become the perfect wife for a man a lot like himself), even now when it was becoming less and less likely that I'd ever come around, I was still his best girl, the apple of his eye.

Feeling more confident than I had in years, I called my parents and asked for their opinions on some serious legal and medical matters. Things seemed to be going well until my mother got off the phone to take another call and my father said, "Look, we've been dealing with this and will continue to, but I want you to know what a great disappointment it is."

I couldn't speak. Having always found my father's disappointment impossible to bear, I grunted a good-bye, hung up, and burst into tears.

A few minutes later the phone rang—my mother wanting to make sure I was all right. As we continued to talk, my mother began to speak of that Mother's Day when I was about six, maybe eight, and we went out for lunch at Tavern on the Green. Did I remember?

Yes, I said, I remembered (unless I was just remembering because she'd mentioned this not too long ago, shortly after I'd sent her a book that included a section on lesbian daughters coming out to their mothers—a section she said she found very moving). I remembered the lushness of Central Park, the horse-drawn carriages, the tables with linen cloths and pink flowers, the ladies with their pastel dresses, men in their dark suits, the roving violinists. And yes, I remembered what my mother most remembered: how I sat in my party dress with my legs wide apart, absolutely transfixed by the couples dancing. Once again, as my mother spoke of this, she choked up, and, lumpy-throated myself, I wondered just what was causing our emotion. Not the wide-apart legs adumbrating lesbianism—no, I'd always been, still was, on the feminine side—more likely it was that she could not find the thread connecting that little girl to the woman I've become, or even if she could (and once or twice she suggested an intuitive understanding of why a woman might choose a woman), it saddened her that I was never going to be a part of those handsome couples that so entranced me.

Later that night I watched "Eyes on the Prize" on TV. There were Andrew Goodman's parents talking about him with pride and continued belief in his cause. There was Medgar Evers's wife just after her husband was killed by white supremacists. There was Fannie Lou Hamer, a poor uneducated woman speaking out so passionately, so articulately. All that hope and dignity, unity and courage—it moved me so, that night especially because it was my disappointed father who had taught me about Rosa Parks and *Brown* v. *Board of Education* and had told me, again and again, how important it is to stand up for what you believe in.

The next morning, crossing the river in the ancient BMW my father had handed down to me, I heard Yehudi Menuhin playing Brahms's Violin Concerto, one of my father's favorites. Turning onto Storrow Drive I switched into fourth, and amidst the rising curlicue of strings I discovered I was crying yet again—from the memory of that music filling the house of my childhood, the order, the sunlight, the passion, the faith in the future.

A month later Jim and I met in a Mexican restaurant to discuss our wishes—those we'd agree on informally and those we'd put into a legal contract. How much should he see the child? How much should he pay? What if the child isn't normal? What if Jim marries and has other children? Should he be present at the birth? And just what is it I'm afraid of—too much involvement or not enough?

The answer: both.

That summer, Fred Astaire died. I heard the news on the radio and gasped. I'd always loved Fred; still, that didn't explain the grief I felt. On the radio they called it "the end of an era, the end of style, of dancing cheek to cheek."

In October 1987 I attended the gay rights march on Washington with Karen. I knew that if I ever did have a child, this would at times mask my lesbianism, at other times expose it. I knew it was important for my child as well as myself that I—Dale and I—be proud of who we are. Walking through a city overtaken by gay people, doing my habitual accounting of ways I was and was not like other gay people—I couldn't help noticing what seemed to be a particularly high proportion of people of both genders wearing red glasses. I wore red glasses, and I loved my red glasses, had always felt they were "me"; so maybe that's what clinched it—all those red glasses: I was glad to be there, I identified, I belonged. I felt that way even at the mass gay wedding, a lengthy, hodgepodge ceremony full of Christian and pantheistic rhetoric, liberation politics, flowers, and kitsch, where all the very weirdest had gathered—the fattest, skinniest, hairiest, smoothest, queens, bull dykes, down-and-outest—even there I felt at home, like this was the appropriate, the logical place for me to be, given everything I was—a New York Jew, a graduate of a college known for its radical politics, a writer, my father's daughter, my mother's daughter. For old time's sake and for ongoing friendship, Karen and I married. We didn't have a ring, but we kissed; we threw rice.

A journal entry from late August 1988: "Last night I checked my mucous—stretchy. Jim called to say we're on for Saturday.

Last session with M. helped me decide on AI as opposed to intercourse. It's more important for Dale to be there and in on this from the very beginning. I picture us making love first and me crying—for a change. But I can also imagine feeling happy, close, excited. And Labor Day weekend—how auspicious!"

What actually happened: It poured on our way to Vermont, but just as we drove up to Jim's funky farmhouse, the sun peeked out. On the oak kitchen table were pink and violet wild-flowers. Jim appeared with a bottle of champagne. He took out the crystal glasses, and we sipped to I don't remember what. Soon after, Jim disappeared into his room and we sat out back with Coney. In ten minutes, maybe fifteen (it was beginning to seem like Jim might be running into difficulties), he walked out the back door and stuck up his thumb. We cheered. Dale and I (and Coney) headed into his cool, damp bedroom with its brass bed, white comforter, tree-graced window. The glass was on the night table, the sperm pearly, ample. I had my syringes (sans needles). Never very dexterous, I fumbled through the procedure. No time to make love even if we'd been so inclined. I suppose I had imagined Dale inserting it, in some pathetic imitation of intercourse, but she didn't want to. So I did it. And then, we waited the requisite twenty minutes, urging the miracle to occur.

It didn't.

Not that time. Nor the next few. But one Thursday after-noon in November (Veterans Day!) I drove up by myself feeling something in the air. Jim wasn't home yet when I arrived, and I'd had such a heady trip I took out my notebook and began writing:

I will call you A for beginning, and will tell you how it was—the ride up to Vermont for your conception. Late fall. Still filled with ambivalence, I imagined turning around— but midway or so, my mood changed. I saw men in their cars

The Death of Fred Astaire   153

glancing at me and couldn't help feeling pleased. I heard Dvořák's American Quartet—long lines, full of melancholy and longing. Maybe that was it, or the wind picking up. I felt a tenderness for this crazy life of mine. I imagined I was going up to see my lover to make a baby, you. Then, remembering it wasn't like that, I imagined how, many years from now, I would describe the night you were conceived. Funny I never asked my parents about my conception. Never asked my mother if she had any misgivings, and if she did, I'm not sure I'd want to know. But if you want to know whether you were born of love: you were. I think that's what I'm trying to say. Tonight I loved my life—the music, the sky, the journey, the freedom. I stopped for gas. Self-service was crowded so I splurged. I stopped to buy wine for later, coffee for now. It started to rain. I almost missed my exit. I felt a pain, near my right hip, thought I might be ovulating that very minute. Touched my breasts—not swollen yet. Threw my quarters into the basket and one fell. I thought about telling you all these little things. Stories with no point except that I had a life. I was here. It was ordinary and I was caressing it all— the ordinary, the strange, the way it was and wasn't what I wanted. I wanted you to know you had a mother who drove to Vermont, stopped for gas, wine, coffee, almost missed her exit, got teary-eyed with Dvořák and thoughts of you. Men looked at her, and she felt right in the middle of her life. She listened to the radio. "One quarter of the New York prisoners have AIDS. Texas will be the site for the $4.4 billion atom smasher. Bush, elected two days ago, is working to smooth out his transition to the White House." No, the world isn't going the way I'd like. Even my life—not the way I imagined. Harder. But I headed north off the highway. It got dark and began to rain. At Route 107, I made a sharp right, and there was Anabel's, a white colonial inn, all lit up. And somehow that was enough—sublime. And you.

I realize now I've been thinking of you as a boy.

Two dogs are curled up beside me now in front of the woodstove. Dale is home. I called her earlier. We had a nice talk. You are on your way.

And he was.

This is not, of course, the end of the story. That boy is now almost two, and there's much I could say about how it has been and how our unusual family puts us both on the margins of conventional society and, at the same time, smack in the middle of it. But I must stop soon. And in searching for a way to close, I remember a recent fantasy: It's Mother's Day years from now. We go to Tavern on the Green or some place like it, and Max sits with his knees apart and, enchanted, watches his two moms dance.

But who am I kidding. Even if Dale were the type, even if it became perfectly acceptable for two women to slow dance at Tavern on the Green—it's not just the dance that holds such sway over me. It's the tension between the dress and the suit, the smooth and the rough, the swinger and the one swung.

Or so I thought. Now I'm not sure.

A few weeks ago I went to a concert of ballroom dancers. To my surprise, I found all that cheek-to-cheek stuff rather dull and bloodless. At first I decided this was probably because the men were all gay. Then I read in the program that most of the couples were married (to each other); so I thought, well, maybe *that's* why it's so desexualized. Then the tangos began: first women tangoing with women, then men tangoing with men. (I leaned forward in my chair and sat with my legs apart, entranced.) And afterward even the straight woman I was with agreed this was by far the most exciting number. The odd thing was, nothing seemed odd about it. There was no cross-dressing; the women all wore tight black dresses, the men tight black suits; no partner seemed to lead the other; and yet—how they sizzled!

So who knows?

I write this from a cabin in the country. Here with Dale and Max, we have time and air and mountains. Sometimes we put on Max's red plastic Sony and dance in the kitchen—all three of us or some combination of two or Max alone—and then I catch Dale's eye and we smile and I think, *I'm not missing anything, this is the whole thing.*

from *1935*

The Streets Are Flowing Rivers

The blacks on McCullough Street, Druid Hill Avenue, and Linden Avenue were people of the Depression in Prohibition neighborhoods that Jean Toomer called "the Preacher-Driven Race"—faces that have all faded, all gone now with a quiet dignity, who on many a Sunday morning sang "My Lord What a Morning" and on weekends, before the sun went down, "The Worried Blues Ain't All Bad."

My grandmother, mother, and father were among the people in these small, vanished places. To walk through these streets is not to see the people that stare out of the darkness of memory, or return at dusk, or speak from photographs and fading letters found in some half-hidden place where my grandmother, grim and forbidding in long, flowing dresses, and my mother, shy in her wide, dark clothing, went off to work. My mother was a heavy brown woman whom I see each day in the supermarket line or struggling to step into the bus. She limped a little bit, and like my brother, her oldest son, she had a mean temper when offended.

Way
down South
my weary memory
goes   the voice
of the Negro
is like poetry   the Bible fading
on the shelf

my mother every
day
polished her floors
like a precious gift
but in church she wept
in the palms
of her hands
for more

The Folks at Home

Grandmother Keyes. When she came to the door I was afraid
to kiss her. After all, I was a boy. She would touch my head,
saying I needed a haircut. My heart beat loudly when I came
into her dark rooms.

Grandmother Nichols. A woman sitting on a porch, stiff and
still, almost afraid to smile, her hands dropped into her lap.
Her face in shadow was black as the unlit corners of the house,
her hair white as straw. There is a picture of our house, the
screen door opening up on the darkness of the hallway and the
beginnings of a staircase.

Father. My mother always said that to see me was to see
my deceased father coming into the house. His mustache was
like the handles on a bicycle. My mother would say, "Your
father died after you were born and when you would cry he hit
you on the bottom." She asked me if I remembered him and I
said, "No!"

Uncle Herbert. A pale working Memphis soul, he smelled
of rye whiskey, a five-cent cigar wrapped in gold, and hard
work. He had the thin mustache of a Sweet Man. The ladies
loved him; he carried a hernia through middle age. He was a
drinking man and for years was the man I watched because
I grew in his shadow: churchgoing people would call him "a
lazy niggerman, sleeping in his clothes."

In Baltimore, where a Negro gardener named George Baker, or "Father Divine," once shouted, "I am God," there is also Druid Hill Avenue, which is shaded by large oak trees, and sidewalks of lemon-colored Negroes in front of their brown-stones (abandoned side-street row houses and shacks)—full-lipped darkies with hair dense as the fabled jungles of Africa, dark and loving skin ("lak dusk when you sing") who call each other "nigger." In the afternoon glow, they "travel light," as the song goes, but in life they sing, "My heart is broke and it won't ever mend." Their songs are the blues of women treated awful and the men who cheat them, beat them: "I knows the men don't like me because I speaks my mind." The old men talk of old whites who used to live there when the neighbor-hood was upper middle class and huge chandeliers hung in the hallways where the "uppity" Negro schoolteachers live. It is cold for the old men huddled in hoods in the vestibules.

In the quiet street of the Depression years ("the shipyard's shut down and rent day's coming and what I hear is that the landlord's got the blues"), the corner store gives credit: five cents' worth of coal oil, fifteen cents' worth of bologna, a little fatback for the lima beans. Some of the out-of-work sleep so hard, because you drink so much whiskey when you are down . . . Aunt Harriet's friend Uncle Eddie brings butter beans and chicken to fry and a bright golden smile ("in our hungry times we got Joe Louis"). Uncle Eddie loves Little Lulu.

Eddie is a laugh and fine
shoes
full lips and white
teeth grinning
to high
heaven
Eddie from Georgia   sorrowful place

for a Negro

lived in one room played numbers keeping
the figures in his head
Eddie was sweet-smelling life
Dixie Peach and after-shave
     handsome as
a preacher's suit and as dark   never
attended People's Baptist
God (Eddie said)
made Sunday for fried chicken
and reading the comic pages
of the *Baltimore Sun*

My mother pulling (she calls it combing) my hair for Sunday, yanking it a little, it being so nappy, and reading Mother Goose—stories of weeping queens by their fountains dreaming of young blond men, choirs of angels dressed in white coming for the dying Uncle Tom, southern rabbits with the lively tongues of slaves. My uncle Herbert told me about chain gangs (worse than trouble all day long); my grandmother and churches had words about the Army of the Lord (which I supposed my hair was being cut for). But when Eddie, a wonderful greasy brown man, came for his weekly visit, he read stories about Red Barry, a crime fighter, an undercover cop with guns that blazed like cannons: "Bang! Bang! Bang!"

I was born in a house without gas or electricity where for fifteen years the only hot water was boiled on a stove that heated water in a bucket over a wood fire, and the lights would be the dim lamp that sat on the kitchen table. It was a house lit by wood and coal oil. The winters were so cold that the toilets froze under us. My brother and I would take long walks through these emptied streets of windowed, shuttered houses looking for newspapers, through the smoke of passing trains, streets already black with soot, narrow streets where bundles of newspapers were left on the curb. Rats squeaked in the night and mice walked in the kitchen looking for food as we children looked for candy. In the streets men dug in the dust of their pockets to fool themselves. The winter was so cold the fingers broke off and the hand hung there.

As young children my brother and I slept between my mother and grandmother, and when we were older I slept with my brother. I wrote about him in my first book, in a poem entitled "My Brother Is Homemade." I was eager for my grandmother to sleep beside me, although many times I waked in the night, fearing she had died in her sleep because she was so much older than me. I was relieved to hear her breathing beside me. By the time I was going on eight or nine, I had long since been sleeping with my brother but always missed being beside my grandmother in the night.

My grandmother was a "yellow woman," a fair-skinned woman who the neighbors said acted like a visiting white lady from the big house. She was hard on children who picked their noses and didn't wipe after leaving the toilet, but most of all she believed that the devil would get you if you fucked around too much. It was a life of poverty: she made never more than fifteen to twenty dollars a week in her life, and she worked until she could no longer wash floors or scrub walls. She complained and wanted better for herself but worked nevertheless, and when she couldn't do it anymore, we lived—if we were lucky—on welfare. One year we were fortunate because my mother got a job with the post office and for a time our clothes were new and food was more plentiful.

We slept in the cold, with all the doors of the house pulled shut, the walls and windows stuffed with cloth or newspapers, the rat holes nailed up with tin from vegetable cans. The rooms were dimly lit by an oil lamp after dark, when the shades were drawn, a timid flame burning inside the darkening globe. We lived in this apartment for fifteen years, and one of my most vivid memories was when my grandmother visited my aunt for a while and I had decided to spend New Year's with my mother. When the firecrackers went off in the street, I was sitting on my mother's bed reading *Paradise Lost*, surprised to find it not difficult but interesting enough to read, and smiled as my mother looked fondly at me. Although I knew my brother was out in the street with a gang of tough older boys, perhaps drinking peach or apple wine, or even getting laid in some dark hallway (standing up), I also knew that he had started me to read years ago.

My brother is homemade
like he was first real
black boy I ever knew

before Richard Wright
or James Baldwin found
black summers
he taught me how to drink
at age five and a half
& cleaned the streets
with bullies and stolen
bread and ice cream

he came into this color
thing
lighter than most
& so to prove a point
grew darker than most

The World of Boys in a Box of Books

He may be dead, and by now perhaps he is: older brothers have so much to prove to neighborhoods of boys. They will lie about how bad they are and how much wine they can drink, stealing loaves of bread, swiping nickels in the schoolyards, duking it out in front of the chicks, swinging a mean fist behind his back, approaching the big bad city with a strut, like a man, like a dude.

Herman Cornish liked to read (even if he was a badass dude) "Batman, the eerie nemesis"—he would stumble here—"of crime." Big words on the pages of illustrated noir, illustrated comics. This is not the America of Walt Disney: Batman's was a dark world, closer to the hard-bitten tales of Dashiell Hammett and Scarface. The Joker was a green-haired white man; Batman was a vampire living for the night to prey upon the city, the living dead Nosferatu in pursuit of a common thief Joe Chill: "I'll never stop hounding you!" he threatened Chill, who never forgot the vengeful eyes of young Bruce Wayne after he gunned down the boy's parents on a grim night many years before in Gotham City. Now Chill was an old man in a cold sweat, white-haired and trembling at the sight of the monster he inadvertently created: a creature that both law-abiding citizens and members of the underworld alike saw as the devil stalking the eerie night of what was then (and now) called Gotham/New York City.

Herman Cornish loved books.

In the winter of that year when FDR was still president, hoboes were knocking at the door asking for something, anything, to eat. Men and women were crowded in boxcars, sometimes as many as sixty people fleeing riots, strikes, and union breakers, the gray flatlands and the black storms. My brother steals a book. Books were spread over the kitchen tablecloth: stories of southern lynch mobs, Negro men learning the hard lessons of Jim Crow, the endless voyages of Ulysses. He steals a box of magazines from the newspaper truck: "How Strong Is Japan?" *Life* magazine asked us from the kitchen table. Japan's army looks "sloppy, dirty and stupid," we read, and a white man tells us, "My wife knows I can't build fighting ships on sissy food."

In my room, with the bed against the wall so I could look out of the window, I had comic books stacked neatly in a corner and a closet door that always came open at night. There was a bureau drawer with the paperbacks by Raymond Chandler, *Saturday Evening Post* short stories, western novels by Max Brand, *The Scourge of the Rio Grande*, by Evan Evans: "A red-faced man who walked with a slight limp came through a patch of misty light and into shadow . . ."

At four-thirty, when lamps were lit but throughout the country the lights were out, some blues men still sang. They would rather drink "muddy water" than live in cities—the brown and dusty land, Georgia, South Carolina, the shines, the coons, where there's nothing but the rock to call out, "no hiding place." As with most members of my generation, there was a Harlem of the mind, with its music and mulattoes, overcooked and overseasoned soul food, and the politics of the early 1930s . . . a song.

"Strange Fruit," a song from the soul of Billie Holiday, spoke of "black bodies swinging in the southern breeze," the Deep South and the dark glow of the Negress in her cabin, the dark men alive in northern Cadillacs, Prohibition, and my dead father; strange fruit that death seemed to wait for in open darkness and uncertain daylight. Billie's song was heard in the northern cities and "hanging from the poplar trees" sung in Harlem and other Harlems across the urban North: strange fruit black song in a white country . . .

Negro Collage

Cab Calloway, Negro entertainer and "Master of Hidey Ho," was a musician with hair shined black—what my mother called "good hair"—shined like coal oil, long, hiding his face when he strutted and shook it, his windy voice throbbing like a congo drum. Those long strands of wild and perfect Negro hair in 1935. In Harlem in those days, the Afro haircut was a "disgrace." Barbers stood in front of their shops and, with nervous and anxious fingers, broke open and shut their scissors, combs in their back pockets and no money in their front pockets. But they loved it when Cab Calloway and Louis Armstrong came uptown and performed for the folks (putting on a "little congo" in the street); a shantytown and down-home blues on weekend nights when people went really wild, but more importantly, to move those cans of hair straightener and promote good barbering. Otherwise it was played for white people in those clubs that Negroes could only experience by sitting in the balcony of the local segregated movie house and in the Negro theaters, which were always named after presidents: Washington, Lincoln, Jefferson, Madison, and, of course, the Roosevelt.

In the days of "good" and "bad" hair, entertainers burned their scalps to make their hair like silk and tar—cool jigaboos wailing and thrusting the head: Cab with his baton, conducting the orchestra as though it were a minor inconvenience, a mere background noise getting in the way of his voice as he wailed and complained about "Minnie the Moocher."

Harlem was Cab Calloway and Harlem was the Negro to me. I thought of Harlem then like younger poets dream of Africa. What a woman did to Cab, where railroad men like Paul Robeson's Redcap Jones came for cards, fighting lightskinned mamas singing blues and wearing red, where he felt like a man instead of a mule. Cotton was down South, and all life was like a Sunday with your best shoes, suits, and dresses on.

Harlem is the Negro's *there:* Harlem my down-home themes in the urban North, city of Hidey-Hidey-Ho and rent parties. Langston Hughes and the Renaissance. I can see old Cab dressed in a white coat, shirt, and tails prancing back and forth, smile bright enough to make you color-blind.

One more time, Cab, "Hidey, Hidey Ho!"
for this city

Harlem Promenade

Stepin Fetchit
a fool
won't work but will
fish
and sleep
roll his   eyes   let the whites show
his dark head
says
my soul
is satisfied
um-huh like an ol' blk snake
would move
but rather sit
down
or steal
chickens
this   friend of old
Judge Priest
Stepin Fetchit
a dope-
pusher sitting in
a balcony
in the Cotton Club   thinks   he's   a bad
nigger lovin
fat women

1935—darktown coaltown Burma Road   a mean wind
blows
&   this morning

           on the avenue
like old
        Jim Crow   & hard times   pockets
full
    of pain
country boys   badass
        Uncle
Toms
good
for
a mugging
are the people
barricaded in rib shops,
music stores
Sambos
with busted heads
        and purple-lipped
high as a Georgia pine
      are the people

     Louis Armstrong (inferior handkerchief
head full of Vaseline
instead of shit)

the Sons of Hams slop
hogs
& drink
               draw water
from the streams
and wells,
      live in the slums
of the cities,
the shacks in the rural towns and country
suffer conjure women
the Sons of Ham disease and poverty,

voodoo in a porkpie hat
show stoppers
like Bojangles,
holy ghost in the front yard
Jelly Roll on the street corner
the people of the inferior races
the children of Ham
"for the sun to rot"
that   evening sun
Southern trees "here is a strange and bitter cry"
        song of
                young Billie a voice like the Southern
dusk remembered
high brown face burned by the sun
on a sinful road
        and these   white men
who took her lord away
        "here is a fruit for the crows to pluck"
sang
        Billie

Tragic Ground
(after Erskine Caldwell)
his
farmers
crackers
Okies
poor
white pecker-
woods
never listened
to the "Fanfare
for the Common
Man" (or endured Aaron Copeland)

saw the ribs
through the hides
of their cattle
& kicked their mules

Their children froze in one-room schoolhouses, learned the Bible, despised communism and Jews. In the cities, white men leapt from windows and hungry men walked the streets. Corn burned in 1933, people were threatened for feeding Negroes at the back door, men went to the brown fields, some white boys learned to shoot craps like niggers and were brown from the sun and dark gray from the dust that fell and drifted on them. Men of the soil who could drive for miles in a hungry land of tambourines and gospel gone bad—that lonesome valley. Now you have got to walk it by yourself in a white man's world.

Nobody else can walk it for you except herds of nigger women.

Now listen to the noble farmers in Walker Evans's photographs, the Okies of Steinbeck, and the proud ethnic white women of Dorothea Lange. The terrible Dixie sun morning on the chain gang and the afternoon pounding like a hammer.

Listen to them.

Nigger this and nigger that, and they will tell you it was those Jews that made that nigger bad, education that made him not fit to live with.

Worked from dark into morning into dusk year after year and never went anywhere unless it was to town and sat on the steps outside the general store in a simpler time. A store that sold candies called "nigger babies" had now only a field where a cornstalk remained after the grasshoppers had passed over the land; these men who suffered drought, fought in the Great War, loved baseball, and never visited New York but lived with winter's hunger rocking in a chair, sweeping the barns. Shooting niggers and calling Roosevelt a fucking hypocrite.

1935
there's trust 7 white
men in white
shirts
their bellies hanging
like old women
out of a shanty
watching
the haze
over the scorched fields
1935
there's trust and niggers
bagging
cotton
and a midwife
muttering
to the house
where I was born

Good people prayed at tables when meals were simple and life was hard work. This was the America of the swimming hole and the Scottsboro boys, Sacco and Vanzetti, courthouses where you swapped horses. These people of America sat around all day in the Heartland, in the Deep South. Rode mules and returned full of the spirit, the soul in the stiff collars or overalls. These people of Chattanooga where the freight trains passed through and little white boys threw stones at the Negroes who rode the rails and slept in hobo "jungles." In town, they pointed a gun at the freight train, and as the serious southern talk began and the youngest of the Negro boys began to cry, a deputy flashed a badge, his gun, and began to smile ("blood on the leaves") in the year 1935.

Once when there were poor men, wife and children and a great poverty and hunger in the land, black storms fell upon the land, wind swept the cities and the sun burned the earth until it was brittle and dark, like a cake left too long in the oven, a man tossed in his bed and said to his wife, "What is to become of us?"

Rising Sun

Harlem loses its temper.

1935. The word is in the papers, on the lips of Americans. This is the spring of the "Brown Bomber": twenty-one-year-old Joe Louis, who has spent nine thousand dollars buying a house for his mother and who is driving a car. In the gym where Joe works out, he is a champ. In the ring, he knocks them out by the third round. Opponent Great Lazer, a shattered man, goes down onto the canvas, Louis makes twenty thousand; other men of his race sleep the cold night in boxcars, whisper in barbershops, "ol' Joe," with the fear and black anger of the Negro people in his fist. But newsmen and cameramen fight to interview him, to take his picture. He is onstage at the Harlem Opera House, "a good boy," a symbol for his people: when the Brown Bomber steps into the ring, he brings the Negro millions, the Bible and the judgment of the Good Book in his terrible fists to pummel the white man. He has climbed trees for photographers, eaten large pieces of steak, demolished punching bags. Black people drive out from Harlem to Louis's training camp. When Louis lands a punch, it is like the shouting of the preacher in church, a minister on fire.

In this world of Negro shacks and unemployment, southern men and women in flight from the boll weevil and King Cotton are now stuffed into northern urban ghettos. It is the romance of the song: "I stood outside the gate, steal away, no more trouble, sometimes I wring my hands and cry, cry, cry. Precious hog meat helps me sing, let me live, I slaughter the pig because I don't want to go to Heaven. Oh, sometimes I am troubled all day long." It is Jack Kerouac looking for Negro girls. It is Allen Ginsberg listening to jazz. I wondered what the Beats were looking for in those dreadful streets. Sure not the voice of the Negro of the cane field or factory, but the Negro with his dice and fine long mamas, sweet as a lollipop, and the fathers and sons who traveled in boxcars south and boxcars north. Scottsboro southern boys riding the rails like Ginsberg's Jews and hipsters. In *Howl*, Ginsberg touches, however briefly, on the relationship between Negro and Jew. Kerouac, in his wanderings across America, saw the beauty the Negro refused to see. The beauty that Kerouac and Ginsberg sought in the streets and highways, in the jazz and blues, although what they found was only a vast and lonely landscape inside themselves.

Old neighborhoods: the Negro streets, anger for the beat poet Allen Ginsberg and salvation for beat novelist and travel writer Jack Kerouac where jazz and the beauty of Negro women were forbidden and alluring. A city within a city, a church in the middle of the black chanting the words of the hymn, "Leaning on the Everlasting Arms," and rows of cars lining the street. On the sidewalks, respectable Negro families, maids and bellhops, redcaps and schoolteachers, faces clean and polished, gleam like sunshine and brightly washed windows, dark as smoke. During the week they speak of other things: other Negro boxers, or Bomber's Bob Scanlon, a former cowboy, the second cook on a ship headed for England, who did so by replacing another colored fighter, Frank Craig, a middleweight of his time, all-brown bantamweight champion.

With pride, my grandmother speaks of the voice and presence of Marian Anderson singing, "I got a hiding place in the Word."

1935, and the lady sings the blues, wants the world to know what the blues is all about: the shortage of Negro jobs. Railroad workers and ministers are attacked by white mobs. Negro youth are unemployed. While it is accepted that the Negro has always lived in a depressed United States, even the nigger jobs and life-styles are threatened. Negro miners are attacked by white gangs who feel the loss of their jobs. They say unions continue to close their doors. Negro farmers in the South lose over four million acres of land, the separate and unequal schools deteriorate, lynch mobs continue to gather. Mobs of townspeople—not rednecks or the fat-necked sheriffs of southern fiction, but decent people, ordinary citizens—deny the rights of the Negro as Congress looks away from antilynching laws, the numerous deaths in Mississippi and Georgia, the hallways and streets of Chicago, the Harlems of the United States, the Harlem in New York. Fascism in Ethiopia. It does not matter if Ethiopians consider themselves anything but American Negroes with slave names, history of poverty, emancipation, and servitude. Ethiopia, the Jim Crow laws, the slaughtering of Negro troops after the First World War in the cities and the southwestern state of Texas, the bloody Chicago riots, the shame of the Gold Star mothers forced to travel in Jim Crow ships to visit the graves of Negro soldiers slain in the service of their country.

"The Negro must have his country with pride and heroines": Marcus Garvey names a steamship after the eloquent poet Phillis Wheatley. The Negro must organize. What will become of the Negro in five hundred years, said Marcus Garvey. Rise up, you mighty race! You are the words of Frederick Douglass, the deeds of Booker T. Washington, the revolts of Denmark Vesey, Harriet Tubman, the valor of Sojourner Truth, the nationalism of Negro Henry Highland Garnet, the fighting voice and stature of Paul Robeson. You are a force that peeks out of the Jim Crow cars and trains, the laws that separate the people of a nation, the spirit of the Negro churches, the NAACP, the union of sleeping-car porters. All worlds are pulled together in the tragedy of Ethiopia. Rise up, you mighty race!

Of Rice and Bread

My earliest memories include a Japanese-American gentleman of indeterminate age showing me his hands, which had
no thumbs. He made his personal misfortune a lesson in table
manners: "If you don't eat your crusts, you'll lose your thumbs,
like me."

At that time, I didn't think to ask how he, a rice eater, could
have been forced to eat bread. Neither did I ask if he would
have lost these important appendages had he avoided bread
entirely. Nor did I know at the time that anthropologists such
as Loren Eiseley would identify opposing thumbs as the fea-
ture that distinguishes man from his primate past and from his
oceanic superiors. Man vaulted from the shrieking hordes into
the industrial revolution on the strength of his thumbs. In 1943,
in the midst of a nationalized American concentration camp,
which we who lived there have so blithely labeled "Camp,"
this gentleman was demonstrating the loss of his rights of citi-
zenship by displaying the loss of his thumbs. He was the first
to testify that in America, not eating bread—and breaking it—
resulted in punishment.

In Camp, some of the elders had little to do but sit around
and whittle cartoon characters from some fairy world like Disney's or embroider bluebirds on flowering trees in a land that
barely supported the sagebrush dusting the horizon; others
cleaned latrines or ladled mush in the mess halls. While hardly
patriotic examples of the war effort, these activities filled the
lonely, monotonous days of Camp inmates. In retrospect, even
these simple human activities would have been difficult for one
without thumbs.

I think, as I write this, that his name was Kaz (First Son), the now faceless citizen who so marked my earliest human existence. While he probably lost his thumbs the way many other Asian men lost theirs, plowing fields on the farm or laying rails for the Northern or Southern Pacific, his message has cast dreary sheets of anxiety, apprehension, and even dread over all the choices I've had in life. And it's an effect that I'm afraid has been repeated too many times in camp families. His example seems to speak that breaking rules, even if the rules aren't clear to everyone, may result in swift emasculation, confinement, and loss of personal rights and dignity. Do such effects seem so farfetched? In my family the two most frequent injunctions to the child in the years after our release from Camp were "Be careful" and "What will people say?"

To the ears these words express the normal concerns of a caring mother for her child, yet "being careful" did not always mean watching for cars, nor was "everyone" the Asian-American community alone, but *everyone*, especially those who might be in power. The words I heard whenever I left the house or moved from my mother's side remained the same: "Be careful." Careful of what? Of what I might say to a passing stranger? Of how I might answer the teacher's question? Of what I might do to offend the community or embarrass my parents? Until recently, I found myself interminably considering every decision; and an accidental harm I cause to another weighs on my conscience for days and weeks, even years. The result is that I've lived my life looking over my shoulder, as if to survey the potential damage I might have carelessly and incautiously caused. Even now, some hidden conditioning makes me endlessly weigh the consequences of speaking out in public, until the opportunity passes.

My friend remembers standing at a gate, looking up at a straw-haired young soldier on the other side of the barbed-wire fence, pointing a rifle at her. "Take another step," he says in her nightmares, "and you're dead." The memory is enough, she says, to make her consider every word before she speaks. For her experience speaks caution in every life choice she must make.

For too many Asian Americans, eating bread has become a favorite pastime and symbolizes how well we've shed whatever remnants existed of our grandparents' cultures in exchange for the crusts and taste of the culture in power. I often pause and question my own values. Why have I moved from the inner city to the suburbs to the rural solitude of an island in Puget Sound? Why do I make one choice instead of another? Do those choices come, I wonder, as a result of considered decision-making? Or as the result of invisible internal and external forces tugging at me, who struggles to stay whole?

The Issei (the first, immigrant generation) were tough, outspoken, hardy individuals unwilling to take "no" for an answer, able to find solutions to impossible problems through sheer willpower and pride. My grandfather protested antiyellow laws designed to prevent him from owning his own farm, an act I would not have considered taking even thirty years ago, much less in the climate of the country sixty-five years ago. Yet, failing his protest to overturn the law, he and other farmers like him secured their lands by registering them in the names of their firstborn.

Too many commentators have already noted that today the undistinguished life has become the American Dream and life's central design. As businessmen from Japan are lauded for their ability to adapt American and German know-how into successful business enterprises, so Japanese Americans have likewise adopted their American neighbors' values and traditions. While blacks were exalting their blackness and building racial pride, Japanese Americans were moving out to the suburbs, where they "married out" and thus ultimately minimized their children's visibility and vulnerability. In the suburbs rice became a delicacy and bread the staple.

Breaking bread is an American tradition. From the communal activities of the church to the communal dinner table, breaking bread has meant a sharing of the host or the host's beneficence. And Asian Americans as such have been faulted for being too satisfied in sharing the host's munificence, being satisfied with second in place in society and business.

Shortly after my family's return to the West Coast after World War II, a variety of Japanese Christian churches surrounded Seattle's Buddhist church. These included the Japanese Presbyterian, Blaine Memorial (Japanese) Methodist, Japanese Congregational, St. Peter's Episcopal, and Japanese Baptist churches. I became a Baptist when it turned out that my third-grade neighbor, with whom I spent considerable playing time, was the grandson of the Issei minister of the Japanese Baptist church. So, while many of my acquaintances in junior high school attended the local Buddhist church, I was raised an American Baptist.

As much as Catholics condemned us for being Protestants, so also did our Nisei (the second generation, but the first generation born in the United States) Sunday school teachers condemn our Buddhist neighbors. In fact, the young Buddhist hoodlums who snatched kisses from girls, bragged about their fighting and drinking, swore in public, and acted in defiance of all decency seemed as foreign as those immigrant teenagers from China who used to show up in our grade schools to learn English. And yet, as I look back at them, these hoodlums were the more emancipated of our two groups. They were always bending and breaking rules, satiating their curiosities, while we found ourselves in church sipping grape juice and pretending it was wine, and breaking "bread" and pretending it was a tasty morsel fallen like manna and blessed by the word of God instead of the dry, tasteless wafer that crumbled between our fingers.

In short, our Buddhist nemeses were more rice eaters than bread eaters. As rice eaters, they had remained in the houses of their grandparents—figuratively, if not literally—and were taught to embrace their heritage, which flourished with more than the usual accoutrements of rice and incense and golden figures. I remember my neighbor's grandmother, who honored her deceased husband by chanting daily before a Shinto shrine. In contrast, the only Japanese possessions my parents displayed were Peachboy dolls to celebrate Boy's Day. I remember friends whose Issei and Kibei (American-born Japanese who were educated in Japan as children and returned to the United States) parents spoke Japanese to them as a matter of daily conversation; my parents, on the other hand, spoke Japanese when they wanted to ensure their privacy.

I think now of those Buddhist "hoodlums" as characters with an ability to defy and challenge their peers and their superiors. They were, as I remember them, more full of human curiosity and strength than we who had been taught to condemn them.

As I look back at those years from the vantage of half a century, it seems to me that we spent more energy than was necessary making fun of JOBs (just off the boat) and FOBs (fresh off the boat), denied our straight black hair, used Four Flowers pomade to enrich our hair and its style, established Italian teenage girls (Catholics) as models of pulchritude, became Boy Scouts and earned our merit badges but ignored judo, kendo, odori, and Japanese school, and immersed ourselves in religion, basketball, cars, and girls, in that order.

As teens we were persuaded that God's word provided those of us who lived in the spiritual and emotional wasteland of the urban ghetto with the gift of His grace in much the same way that the Jews were saved from starvation in the Mideastern desert. While we had no desserts on our tables, though we were surrounded by America's riches, through His gift we were given access to the riches of heaven. Thus the evangelical swarm of emotions captured us and freed us from the day-to-day drudgery of parents who were locked in houses that were held together by the strength of the paint on their walls, of parents who served long hours in steam rooms and lobbies and dry cleaning businesses, who labored behind dingy hotel counters and swapped one worn sheet for another on foul mattresses, and who butchered chickens, cleared their guts, and packaged thousands by the hour.

In this context, God's salvation seemed indeed a clear and lucid light. It was the dream we all waited for, winning a place in heaven's emotional lottery for a mere pittance worth of "I believe." And as a natural result, I must have been saved on at least three or more occasions.

Unfortunately, the emotional roller coaster ride provided by touring evangelicals led us to disregard the unselfish daily activities of our minister, the Reverend Emery Andrews, whom we all called Andy. Andy could not be described as the ultimate preacher. Until his last sermon, nothing he spoke from the pulpit was memorable, fresh, or insightful. He lacked the oratorical skills that marked the evangelical Nisei ministers who put JBC on their yearly tour. What Andy did was visit the ill in their homes and rebuild houses in Japan after World War II's devastation. He drove the nursery school children to and from school, led the Boy Scout troop and each year spent weeks in the mountains with troops of boys, and drove the youth group from Seattle to evangelical meetings near Santa Cruz, California, by way of Petaluma chicken farms and the Yosemite Firefalls, which we brickbound city dwellers would never have seen had he not neglected his own family's vacations for our edification and salvation. He recognized that we were people for whom his service would make a significant difference, and his commitment was such that he made countless trips between Seattle and Minidoka (one of the concentration camps, in south central Idaho, where Japanese Americans were interned) during World War II, bearing personal belongings and messages to those imprisoned, and moved his family to Idaho during the war to be near his parishioners. Japanese Americans were more than a mission: we were friends and family, and our welfare was the all-consuming labor of his life. While we teenagers were surrounded by evangelical fervor, Andy demonstrated by deed rather than by word what charity meant. In the 1950s he integrated the church, first with other Caucasian men who came with their Japanese war brides, and then with Hercules Anderson, whose African-Japanese-American family was a first in the church. Herc described himself as a carpenter by trade, a mortician by occupation, and a special education teacher by profession. Late at night Herc carved intricate designs on the large cabinets of the speakers for the organ, and on Sundays he sang in the choir. Since neither he nor I could tell if we were on tune, we stood next to each other as if our combined voices would protect us from the choir director's anguished stare. I never felt, however, that Herc's Japanese wife and children felt as comfortable as he did in our church, which he attended for their sake.

Until this time, the church was basically segregated by its congregation's tacit desire; without being consciously aware of it, Andy was bringing us into the twentieth century. It was much later that I learned another lesson, this time at the expense of this man whom I knew much better than I knew Kaz. Andy was the father figure many of us needed during our teen years. I remember visiting his brother's Modesto ranch one year and spending a weekend luxuriating in the canal that irrigated the property, but I never wondered why Andy's wife and children did not travel with us. I never recognized until his divorce that he had dedicated himself to our achieving successful adulthood at the expense of his own personal life. How were we to discern that each moment of his time was his communion gift to us, his life spread bite-sized through all of our lives?

Most unfortunately, the bread of life cast upon daily troubles was not enough for those who lived by the Word itself and who believed that the Word, and not the life well lived, brought salvation. When Andy's inevitable divorce occurred, the members of the church voted him out of the pulpit for not living the truly Christian life we were told was required by the Bible.

How had this man who had given himself unselfishly for so many decades fallen short of his fellow man's expectations? Merely because of some rule that said that no man should put asunder the ties between a man and his wife? Here he was, a sixty-year-old man whose wife was divorcing him, a man who had baptized, counseled, and buried family members of those in the congregation. They refused when he asked them to invite him back into his own house.

The house of communion fell apart like a house of cards. Bread, which should have been the body of Christ, turned to dry crust on the tongue. We who had been granted heaven had made a hell for one who had lived life marked by dedication, duty, sorrow, understanding, and charity.

Although I could look at the life my parents made for themselves and recognize how unhappy and painful their lives were as they devoted themselves to providing a better and safer life for me, I did not see how their travail had twisted me at twenty years into a cautious, narrow-minded, insensitive, thumbless creature of the dark. Their care and cautiousness had a commendable purpose, but in the process had made me a gang member unable to stand at the most critical point in one man's life and speak a dissenting view, to condemn the hypocrisy of the moment. Now that I've grown older and sedentary I've begun to see what my youth has wrought in me. When I was asked recently what I'd like to do with the rest of my life, I had no answer, for I had been too busy taking life as it came to compile the ingredients necessary to choose what my life would involve in my fiftieth decade.

When I remember the two men, one so dim in memory, the other so dear, I see that Kaz has come to symbolize the losses my parents and other Asian Americans have borne as the result of enduring the prejudices that were fueled by World War II as well as those which had formed their self-image in the preceding half century. On the other hand, Andy actively sought out his life goals and gave himself wholeheartedly to us. Whatever the reasons for his divorce, I'm sure Andy's life choices contributed to it. In this sense, Andy clearly made choices of conscience which I, with my limited perceptions, was unable to appreciate until after his funeral. The funeral itself demonstrated the recognition of the larger Japanese-American community for his life work—the outpouring of Buddhist, Catholic, and other Protestant mourners overwhelmed the capacity of Seattle's largest Baptist church.

Andy's work was no commercial success. His was a private and sacred ministry. It had no easy rewards, no clear boundaries, no popular support. What I applaud is the clarity of choice and vision that was his. He must have recognized that any choice would have its own rewards and losses, and he made his choice with commitment.

As long-term targets of prejudice, we have long passed the time to stop mourning what we've lost; it is time to become assemblers of our own lives. Like bakers adding ingredients to our own recipes, we can have a hand in shaping the taste and weight of who and what we are. The new generations must understand this, for they can move into the future without the same personal perplexities preceding generations have had.

The struggles of our parents and friends like Rev. Andrews have taken us a step up the staircase. If there is a next step in the evolutionary spiral through this new society, it is this: that we raise our children not to be invisible members of the broad society but to be visible and visionary. My friends' children recognize that their life choices need not center on choosing between crusts or rice; nor will they accept whatever commercially baked bran-nirvana the fickle taste of society dictates. Their daughter projects herself as a potential college athlete and medical doctor. To achieve her goals she dedicates herself to bicycling at least forty miles a day and enters weekend competitions in Southern California. At the same time, she takes night classes, works during the day at a research laboratory, and teaches ballet classes on weekends.

While I believe that we who teach and parent must empower the children first to create their personal recipes and then to become the people they envision themselves capable of being, as a parent whose influence has been minimized by a fifteen-year divorce, I struggle with my desire to infuse my children with the self-worth to create and fulfill their personal images and the recognition that our separate lives have made such influence a small gesture. My children have already laid out courses for their lives.

My daughter envisions herself an entrepreneur, whose mix of artistic, practical, and social skills will lead her to the level of financial comfort to which she is accustomed. In order to attain her vision she has enrolled in a program noted for its success in developing clothing designers and production people. And I'm pleased to see that my son has chosen a career doomed to failure unless he can take command of his band members in such a way that they create a plan and are charged with the commitment to fulfill their dream. His success depends as much on his active participation as it does on luck.

When I look closely, I see that they carry the scars of their lives. I see one who is confounded by allergies and provincial tastes and prefers to fast when confronted by a table of rice and chopsticks. The other would probably eat Thai food daily but for the smoldering ulcer she carries within.

Whether one is a rice eater or a bread eater is not so important today. What may be more important is that today one may be neither but a consumer of both. Children today are part of a newer multicultural world. When I look at my own family, whose earliest values included pride in being Japanese and pride in being ethnically "pure," I must smile, for I and my sister have children who range through four different ethnicities. While one view of a multicultural country may be a collection of African-American, Native American, Vietnamese, Chinese, or Italian cultures, tomorrow's world will find all of these ethnic heritages bound into any one child. The days of saying, "I can tell Japanese from Chinese just by looking at a group" are gone. The new model of beauty may be seen in the clothing advertisements now being distributed by the top clothing stores in the nation. As a friend pointed out, the women and children who have been chosen as models are so multicultural as to be racially indistinguishable.

While my children may feel the odd finger of prejudice pointing toward them, they despise those who point and feel pride in who they are, but they do not, as we have so often done, characterize themselves first by their ethnic origins. Their Caucasian friends do not befriend them because they are "interesting" or "exotic" or because they have an unusual heritage but because of some other commonality—mutual music, mutual career interests, or mutual history as products of divorce.

I feel torn between desiring for my children acceptance within what we call a multicultural society and wishing that they had a stronger identification with their Japanese, Chinese, and Filipino heritages. I also recognize that at this time in their lives they could do little more than clothe themselves in their grandparents' culture; for because they have been raised almost solely on McDonald's and Sesame Street, their cultural search would make them just another set of ethnic tourists.

But they have multiple cultures as sources from which to draw wisdom, pride, and knowledge. Perhaps at this moment it's enough that they have recipes for their lives and feel that with enough kneading and working of their talents, their dreams will be within their reach.

Black Hair

There are two kinds of work: one uses the mind and the other uses muscle. As a kid I found out about the latter. I'm thinking of the summer of 1969 when I was a seventeen-year-old runaway who ended up in Glendale, California, working for Valley Tire Factory. To answer an ad in the newspaper I walked miles in the afternoon sun, my stomach slowly knotting on a doughnut that was breakfast, my teeth like bright candles gone yellow.

I walked in the door sweating and feeling ugly because my hair was still stiff from a swim at the Santa Monica beach the day before. Jules, the accountant and part owner, looked droopily through his bifocals at my application and then at me. He tipped his cigar in the ashtray, asked my age as if he didn't believe I was seventeen, but finally, after a moment of silence, said, "Come back tomorrow. Eight-thirty."

I thanked him, left the office, and went around to the chain-link fence to watch the workers heave tires into a bin; others carted uneven stacks of tires on hand trucks. Their faces were black from tire dust, and when they talked—or cussed—their mouths showed a bright pink.

From there I walked up a commercial street, past a cleaners, a motorcycle shop, and a gas station where I washed my face and hands; before leaving I took a bottle that hung on the side of the Coke machine, filled it with water, and stopped it with a scrap of paper and a rubber band.

The next morning I arrived early at work. The assistant foreman, a potbellied Hungarian, showed me a time card and how to punch in. He showed me the Coke machine and the locker room with its slimy shower, and also pointed out the places where I shouldn't go: the ovens where the tires were recapped and the customer service area, which had a slashed couch, a coffee table with greasy magazines, and an ashtray. He introduced me to Tully, a fat man with one ear who worked the buffers that resurfaced the whitewalls. I was handed an apron and a face mask and shown how to use the buffer: lift the tire and center it, inflate it with a foot pedal, press the buffer against the white band until cleaned, and then deflate and blow off the tire with an air hose.

With a paintbrush he stirred a can of industrial preserver. "Then slap this blue stuff on." While he was talking a coworker came up quietly behind him and goosed him with the air hose. Tully jumped as if he had been struck by a bullet and then turned around cussing and cupping his genitals in his hands as the other worker walked away calling out foul names. When Tully turned to me, smiling his gray teeth, I lifted my mouth into a smile because I wanted to get along. He has to be on my side, I thought. He's the one who'll tell the foreman how I'm doing.

I worked carefully that day, setting the tires on the machine as if they were babies, because it was easy to catch a finger in the rim that expanded to inflate the tire. At the day's end we swept up the tire dust and emptied the trash into bins.

At five the workers scattered for their cars and motorcycles while I crossed the street to wash at a burger stand. My hair was stiff with dust and my mouth showed pink against the backdrop of my dirty face. I ordered a hotdog and walked slowly in the direction of the abandoned house where I had stayed the night before. I lay under the trees and within minutes was asleep. When I woke my shoulders were sore, and my eyes burned when I squeezed the lids together.

From the backyard I walked dully through a residential

street, and as evening came on, the TV glare in the living rooms and the headlights of passing cars showed against the blue drift of dusk. I saw two children coming up the street with snow cones, their tongues darting at the packed ice. I saw a boy with a peach and wanted to stop him but felt embarrassed by my hunger. I walked for an hour, only to return and discover the house lit brightly. Behind the fence I heard voices and saw a flashlight poking at the garage door. A man on the back steps mumbled something about the refrigerator to the one with the flashlight.

I waited for them to leave but had the feeling they wouldn't because there was a commotion of furniture being moved. Tired, even more desperate, I started walking again with a great urge to kick things and tear the day from my life. I felt weak and my mind kept drifting because of hunger. I crossed the street to a gas station where I sipped at the water fountain and searched the Coke machine for change. I started walking again, first up a commercial street, then into a residential area where I lay down on someone's lawn and replayed a scene at home—my mother crying at the kitchen table, my stepfather yelling with food in his mouth. They're cruel, I thought, and warned myself that I should never forgive them. How could they do this to me?

When I got up from the lawn it was late. I searched out a place to sleep and found an unlocked car that seemed safe. In the backseat, with my shoes off, I fell asleep but woke up startled about four in the morning when the owner, a nurse on her way to work, opened the door. She got in and was about to start the engine when I raised my head to explain my presence. She screamed so loudly when I said "I'm sorry" that I sprinted from the car with my shoes in hand. Her screams faded, then stopped altogether, as I ran down the block, hid behind a trash bin, and waited for a police siren to sound. Nothing. I crossed the street to a church where I slept stiffly on cardboard in the balcony.

I woke up feeling tired and greasy. It was early and a few streetlights were still lit, the east growing pink with dawn. I washed myself from a garden hose and returned to the church to break into what looked like a kitchen. Paper cups, plastic spoons, a coffee pot littered on a table. I found a box of Nabisco crackers and ate until I was full.

At work I spent the morning at the buffer, but was then told to help Iggy, an old Mexican who was responsible for choosing tires that could be recapped without the risk of exploding at high speeds. Every morning a truck would deliver used tires, and after I unloaded them Iggy would step among the tires to inspect them for punctures and rips on the sidewalls.

With yellow chalk he marked circles and Xs to indicate damage and called out "junk." Tires that could be recapped got a "goody" from Iggy, and I placed them on my hand truck. When I had a stack of eight I kicked the truck at an angle and balanced off to another work area, where Iggy again inspected the tires, scratching Xs and calling out "junk."

Iggy worked only until three in the afternoon, at which time he went to the locker room to wash and shave and to dress in a two-piece suit. When he came out he glowed with a bracelet, watch, rings, and a shiny fountain pen in his breast pocket. His shoes sounded against the asphalt. He was the image of a banker stepping into sunlight with millions on his mind. He said a few low words to workers with whom he was friendly and none to people like me.

I was seventeen, stupid because I couldn't figure out the difference between an F78 14 and a 750 14 at sight. Iggy shook his head when I brought him the wrong tires, especially since I had expressed interest in being his understudy. "Mexican, how can you be so stupid?" he would yell at me, slapping a tire from my hands. But within weeks I learned a lot about tires, from sizes and makes to how they are molded in iron forms to how Valley stole from other companies. Now and then we received a truckload of tires, most of them new or nearly new, and they were taken to our warehouse in the back, where the serial numbers were ground off with a sander. On those days the foreman handed out Cokes and joked with us as we worked to get the numbers off.

Most of the workers were Mexican or black, though a few redneck whites worked there. The base pay was a dollar sixty-five but the average was three dollars. Of the black workers, I knew Sugar Daddy the best. His body carried 250 pounds and armfuls of scars, and he had a long knife that made me jump when he brought it out from his boot without warning. At one time he had been a singer and had cut a record in 1967 called *Love's Chance*, which broke into the R and B charts. But nothing came of it. No big contract, no club dates, no tours. He made very little from record sales, only enough for an operation to pull a steering wheel from his gut when, drunk and mad at a lady friend, he slammed his Mustang into a row of parked cars.

"Touch it," he smiled at me one afternoon as he raised his shirt, his black belly kinked with hair. Scared, I traced the scar that ran from his chest to the left of his belly button, and I was repelled but hid my disgust.

Among the Mexicans I had few friends because I was different, a *pocho* who spoke bad Spanish. At lunch they sat in tires and laughed over burritos, looking up at me to laugh even harder. I also sat in tires while nursing a Coke and felt dirty and sticky because I was still living on the street and had not had a real bath in over a week. Nevertheless, when the border patrol came to round up the nationals, I ran with them as they scrambled for the fence or hid among the tires behind the warehouse. The foreman, who thought I was an undocumented worker, yelled at me to run, to get away. I did just that. At the time it seemed fun because there was no risk, only a goodhearted feeling of hide-and-seek, and besides, it meant an hour away from work on company time. When the police left we came back, and some of the nationals made up stories of how they were almost caught—how they outraced the police. Some of the stories were so convoluted and unconvincing that everyone laughed and shouted "*mentiras*," especially when one described how he overpowered a policeman, took his gun away, and sold the patrol car. We laughed and he laughed, happy to be there to make up such a story.

If work was difficult, so were the nights. I still had not gathered enough money to rent a room, so I spent the nights sleeping in parked cars or in the church balcony. After a week I found a newspaper ad for a room for rent, phoned, and was given directions. Finished with work, I walked the five miles down Mission Road looking back into the traffic with my thumb out. No rides. After eight hours of handling tires I was frightening to drivers, I suppose, since they seldom looked at me; if they did, it was a quick glance. For the next six weeks I would try to hitchhike, but the only person to stop was a Mexican woman who gave me two dollars to take the bus. I told her it was too much and that no bus ran from Mission Road to where I lived, but she insisted that I keep the money and trotted back to her idling car. It must have hurt her to see me day after day walking in the heat and looking very much the dirty Mexican to the many minds that didn't know what it meant to work at hard labor. That woman knew. Her eyes met mine as she opened the car door, and there was a tenderness that was surprisingly true—one for which you wait for years but when it comes it doesn't help. Nothing changes. You continue on in rags, with the sun still above you.

I rented a room from a middle-aged couple whose lives were a mess. She was a schoolteacher and he was a fireman. A perfect setup, I thought. But during my stay there they would argue for hours in their bedroom.

When I rang at the front door both Mr. and Mrs. Van Deusen answered and didn't bother to disguise their shock at how awful I looked. But they let me in all the same. Mrs. Van Deusen showed me around the house, from the kitchen and bathroom to the living room with its grand piano. On her fingers she counted out the house rules as she walked me to my room. It was a girl's room with lace curtains, scenic wallpaper of a Victorian couple enjoying a stroll, a canopied bed, and stuffed animals in a corner. Leaving, she turned and asked if she could do laundry for me. Feeling shy and hurt, I told her no; perhaps the next day. She left and I undressed to take a bath, exhausted as I sat on the edge of the bed probing my aches and my bruised places. With a towel around my waist I hurried down the hallway to the bathroom where Mrs. Van Deusen had set out an additional towel with a tube of shampoo. I ran water into the tub and sat on the closed toilet, watching the steam curl toward the ceiling. When I lowered myself into the tub I felt my body sting. I soaped a washcloth and scrubbed my arms until they lightened, even glowed pink, but I still looked unwashed around my neck and face no matter how hard I rubbed. Back in the room I sat in bed reading a magazine, happy and thinking of no better luxury than a girl's sheets, especially after nearly two weeks of sleeping on cardboard at the church.

I was too tired to sleep, so I sat at the window watching the neighbors move about in pajamas, and, curious about the room, looked through the bureau drawers to search out personal things—snapshots, a messy diary, and a high school yearbook. I looked up the Van Deusen's daughter, Barbara, and studied her face as if I recognized her from my own school —a face that said "promise," "college," "nice clothes in the closet." She was a skater and a member of the German Club; her greatest ambition was to sing at the Hollywood Bowl.

After a while I got into bed, and as I drifted toward sleep I thought about her. In my mind I played a love scene again and again and altered it slightly each time. She comes home from college and at first is indifferent to my presence in her home, but finally I overwhelm her with deep pity when I come home hurt from work, with blood on my shirt. Then there was another version: home from college she is immediately taken with me, in spite of my work-darkened face, and invites me into the family car for a milkshake across town. Later, back at the house, we sit in the living room talking about school until we're so close I'm holding her hand. The truth of the matter was that Barbara did come home for a week but was bitter toward her parents for taking in boarders (two others besides me). During that time she spoke to me only twice: once, while searching the refrigerator, she asked if we had any mustard; the other time she asked if I had seen her car keys.

But it was a place to stay. Work had become more and more difficult. I worked not only with Iggy but also with the assistant foreman, who was in charge of unloading trucks. After they backed in I hopped on top to pass the tires down, bouncing them on the tailgate to give them an extra spring so they would be less difficult to handle on the other end. Each truck was weighted down with more than two hundred tires, each averaging twenty pounds, so that by the time the truck was emptied and swept clean I glistened with sweat and my T-shirt stuck to my body. I blew snot threaded with tire dust onto the asphalt, indifferent to the customers who watched from the waiting room.

The days were dull. I did what there was to do from morning until the bell sounded at five; I tugged, pulled, and cussed at tires until I was listless and my mind drifted and caught on small things, from cold sodas to shoes to stupid talk about what we would do with a million dollars. I remember unloading a truck with Hamp, a black man.

"What's better than a sharp lady?" he asked me as I stood sweaty on a pile of junked tires. "Water. With ice," I said.

He laughed with his mouth open wide. With his fingers he pinched the sweat from his chin and flicked at me. "You be too young, boy. A woman can make you a god."

As a kid I had chopped cotton and picked grapes, so I knew work. I knew the fatigue and the boredom and the feeling that there was a good possibility you might have to do such work for years, if not for a lifetime. In fact, as a kid I had imagined a dark fate: to marry Mexican poor, work Mexican hours, and in the end die a Mexican death, broke and in despair.

But this job at Valley Tire Company confirmed that there was something worse than fieldwork, and I was doing it. We were all doing it, from the foreman to the newcomers like me, and what I felt heaving tires for eight hours a day was felt by everyone—black, Mexican, redneck. We all despised those hours but didn't know what else to do. The workers were unskilled, some undocumented and fearful of deportation, and all struck with uncertainty at what to do with their lives. Although everyone bitched about work, no one left. Some had worked there for twelve years; some had sons working there. Few quit; no one was ever fired. It amazed me that no one gave up when the border patrol jumped from their vans, batons in hand, because I couldn't imagine any work that could be worse—or any life. What was out there, in the world, that made men run for the fence in fear?

Iggy was the only worker who seemed sure of himself. After five hours of "junking," he brushed himself off, cleaned up in the washroom, and came out gleaming with an elegance that humbled the rest of us. Few would look him straight in the eye or talk to him in our usual stupid way because he was so much better. He carried himself as a man should—with Old World "dignity"—while the rest of us muffed our jobs and talked dully about dull things as we worked. From where he worked in his open shed he would now and then watch us with his hands on his hips. He would shake his head and click his tongue in disgust.

The rest of us lived dismally. I often wondered what the others' homes were like; I couldn't imagine that they were much better than our workplace. No one indicated that his outside life was interesting or intriguing. We all looked defeated and contemptible in our filth at the day's end. I imagined the average welcome at home: Rafael, a Mexican national who had worked at Valley for five years, returned to a beaten house full of kids dressed in mismatched clothes and playing kick the can. As for Sugar Daddy, he returned home to a stuffy room where he would read and reread old magazines. He ate potato chips, drank beer, and watched TV. There was no grace in dipping socks into a washbasin where later he would wash his cup and plate.

There was no grace at work. It was all ridicule. The assistant foreman drank Cokes in front of the newcomers as they laced tires in the afternoon sun. Knowing that I had a long walk home, Rudy, the college student, passed me waving and yelling "Hello" as I started down Mission Road on the way home to eat out of cans. Even our plump secretary got into the act by wearing short skirts and flaunting her milky legs. If there was love, it was ugly. I'm thinking of Tully and an older man whose name I can no longer recall fondling one another in the washroom. I had come in cradling a smashed finger to find them pressed together in the shower, their pants undone and partly pulled down. When they saw me they smiled with their pink mouths but didn't bother to push away.

How we arrived at such a place is a mystery to me. Why anyone would stay for years is an even deeper concern. You showed up, but from where? What broken life? What ugly past? The foreman showed you the Coke machine, the washroom, and the yard where you'd work. When you picked up a tire, you were amazed at the black it could give off.

Atlantic City—1955

Two mattresses laid out like slices of toast under the slope of my grandmother's attic, and we lie on them, my brother and I, each with our own dreams. The sheets are pulled around my fully clothed body like a Band-Aid stuck to an injured finger. It is almost sunrise. Time to go to work: anticipation has been my wake-up call since I started fishing on the pier.

I first began to sleep in my clothes when I was nine. My brother had discovered the fishing pier, and he and Dad took me there one night. It must have been August, because the weakfish were around. Just as we baited our hooks with sea worms and strips of squid, a storm came in from the south— dark clouds rolling in like smoke from my uncle Jockey's cigar. Life in Atlantic City, where storms are as common as tourists, had taught me to respect the harshness of nature but not to fear it, and this storm was not going to stop any of us from fishing. Once, my father told me that predator fish feed during storms, and this time he was right. The ocean was a frenzy of bait fish leaping from the larger fish trying to eat them, and we could see, among the rough waves, speckled weakfish feeding near the surface. The pier lights weathered the winds, and we caught fish after fish. Every cast brought a hard strike to our lines, and most times a weakfish or a bluefish heaved over the railing to be placed in the large crate we had found there. As tired as I became, even when the storm abated, I cast out, over and over.

That was five years ago, and even though I am now thirteen, whenever I decide to go fishing I sleep in my clothes. My excitement is heightened by my desire not to wake my parents, who are sleeping on their mattress at the tip of this triangular room, especially my easily angered father. The thrill of being nearly a man, of doing a real man's work, makes sleeping fully dressed, even in the heat of an attic in summer, an adventure.

As I get out of my make-do bed, I recall how easy it used to be to stand straight when I was smaller and the slope wasn't so noticeable. For three summers now my parents have sublet at a meager profit our rented apartment to summer vacationers, and we have had to live here, where I miss my toys left in the closet, my fish tank with my soon-to-give-birth angelfish, and my too-soft bed. But I know that every dollar counts toward our getting by. Shoes in hand, I walk bent over in my socks toward the porthole of a window at the far end of the attic. I stop, as I habitually do each morning, to watch my parents sleep. The deep breathing of my father, who is never without a lit cigarette when he is awake, makes the gentle ins and outs of air from my mother's mouth almost inaudible, and I wonder if they are dreaming of me.

I poke my head out of this one hole of light in the room, looking up to see that the stars forecast a clear day; I'll need no cumbersome rain gear. I hate to wear that thick rubber; in the summertime it raises the humidity as if the space between my body and the coat's lining were a tropical rain forest. The window, unfortunately, faces the city rather than the waves, so I never know what to expect from the sea. For someone who pulls a fishing net for a living, the sky represents only half of the equation. Still, I am grateful that this room, which was never built to house a family, has any window at all. We are like the humidity; the tension of closeness is always here.

I look down at the small strip of rag I tied to my grand-mother's clothesline. It tells me both the direction and the intensity of the wind, and now it is hanging like the tail of a frightened dog, straight down. It looks like it's going to be a scorcher, hot as hell and no wind.

Sometimes my grandmother takes down my makeshift weather predictor when she hangs the clothes out to dry. Every summer I look forward to helping her do the laundry in the old washer in the basement; sometimes I get to turn the handle of the wringer as her fat fingers feed the washed clothes through the rollers. I love to watch the pancakes of cloth come out the other side; big pancakes, like the ones at Mammies on the boardwalk where tourists go for breakfast all day long, and even into the night.

Slowly, I wind my way down the two flights of stairs, still carrying my shoes so as not to wake my three aunts, two uncles, six cousins, or grandmother, on my way to the enormous stark white bathroom. The large tub, held up by four talon legs each holding a baseball, takes up only a small portion of this room. It is always cold here, even on the hottest of summer days. Sometimes I use the small bathroom in the basement to brush my teeth, pee, and put on my shoes, but today I feel rushed.

It is still dark out, but a streetlight fills the kitchen with a mystical glow as I turn the round glass doorknob and open the door at the bottom of the inner staircase. Tall masts with large round bulbs, like giant flowers, illuminate the trolley tracks that run behind the house. Big trollies with magnificent straw seats and porcelain loops for holding on. I like to put pennies on the tracks and wait for the heaviness of the trolley to flatten them to quarter-sized wafers. Sometimes they stick to the wheels and are lost forever, but those I do retrive I sell as oddities to the tourists who also buy my painted clamshells and popsicle-stick rafts. I started making my own spending money when I was eight by separating bottles into wooden crates in the back of a hotdog stand on the boardwalk. Since then, I save my coins in a glass jar and I buy comics, candy, and soda whenever I want. My paycheck is not mine to spend. I give it whole to my father. The leftover bread, as usual, is cloth-covered on the kitchen table next to the huge silver knife used to cut it. Two slices will do me until the concession stand on the pier opens, and I can eat donuts and drink coffee with the men while we talk about baseball, fish, and the weather. I like to listen while some of the younger men talk about women or tell jokes which I laugh at but often don't understand.

I need only to go to the cellar where the extra icebox holds my most important secret: worms. Not earthworms, but blood-worms from the rocky shores of Maine. They were purchased fresh yesterday, since no bait shop opens this early; they come in a white Chinese-food container filled with sea grass. A dozen worms, each with a head equipped with four nasty barbs not to be taken lightly.

Knapsack over my shoulder, I open the large front door with its ornate glass and step into the crisp sea air. There really is nothing quite like the first smell of morning at this hour. The salt blankets this Queen of Resorts like fairy dust. Breathing is easy; everything seems fresh and smells sweet like seaweed. I feel fortunate on mornings like this to live in Atlantic City, a place that never really sleeps. There is always a bar closing somewhere, tired women going home to wash off someone else's sweat, a drunk still conscious enough to wave down a jitney, those small buses that run up and down Pacific Avenue; miniature arks amidst the flood of too many people. I never feel alone.

I feel very much a man. Here I am up and going to work when other boys my age are sleeping. This is the hour for adults only, and I'm walking down New Hampshire Avenue to the jitney. I always consider myself lucky, especially as I pass the place where Luke and his father live. Luke was a high school football player who broke his back twelve years ago after being hit in the air while trying to catch a pass. I don't know exactly how it happened, but he hasn't been able to move a single part of his body ever since. He can sort of smile, and he blinks twice for "yes" and once for "no" when I ask him questions. I love to sit with him, opening and closing his fingers as he sits in his old wooden wheelchair, and I tell him stories about fishing. Sometimes other kids make fun of me for even touching Luke, but I don't care. He's my friend, and even though I don't even remember how I started spending time with him, I am his only friend. I wish that someday he would just open those fingers all by himself.

The ride on the jitney from the inlet to Arkansas (pronounced are-CAN-zis in Atlantic City) Avenue is always short on these mornings. From my sack I take the white sailor's parka purchased for a dollar from a man who preferred wine to warmth. This marvelous sailcloth always makes me feel like a great fisherman who catches giant ocean fish. And as I walk the long block to the pier I imagine fishing from one of those boats built for angling; the ones with long noses in the front so men can walk out and harpoon sharks, tuna, or billfish. I am the man inching his way along the narrow gangplank waiting for just the right moment to throw the barb-headed weapon into the heart of the beautiful blue marlin, exhausted and side-up after its struggle with the hook still caught in its mouth. I, in my white sailcloth, am man enough to kill.

Finally I reach the boardwalk, its shops closed by iron shades and covered with a fog more mysterious than the rip-off auction houses, or the places that sell saltwater taffy, which doesn't contain salt water, or even the beach itself, where tourists tan themselves to colors they otherwise despise.

Directly across the boardwalk is the Million Dollar Pier. Built at the turn of the century by one Captain Young, whose magnificent house was once at the very entrance to the pier, it is now home to carnival booths, an Italian village, where I can get my fortune read for a quarter, and, at the very end, the fishing spot; a half mile of tar-coated pilings pounded deeply into the sand with a forest of planks nailed on top to make this a pier. I marvel at the sense of walking on water as I make my way to the net haul at the very end.

I'm usually the first to get there, and today's no exception. I open the locker, grab the fishing rod I made just last winter from a single piece of fiberglass, bait my line, and cast out. I loosen the drag and set the clicking device on my reel, then lean my pole against the railing. This way I can leave my rod alone and hear my line going out if a fish takes my bait, and at the same time go about my job of repairing the net. I imagine the pier from the sky looks like a big letter *J*, and the net hangs just below the surface of the water at the point where the letter curves on the inside.

I stand there in the quiet, watching some of the trapped fish search for a way out. They seem so tranquil even in their bewilderment, swimming easily to the surface and then down again. I wonder what they are thinking as one after another shows a quick glimpse of itself. When I look up I notice several of the regulars coming out to fish. It won't be until eight when the men from Barbera's Fish Market come out in their truck to pull the net, so I have some time to fish, repair any holes in the net with a large wooden needle and thick cotton thread, check the ropes for tangles, and talk with the other fishermen. During calm days like today there is little work to be done.

Fishing is slow today—a few kingfish caught closer to shore by Clarence, who seems always to know where the fish are. A skate is also brought up, and I watch its raylike wings being cut off for fish stew. I know it must be near eight because I hear the sound of the pickup truck's engine, and I look around to see the big Italian men driving too quickly toward me. The fish market's name on the side of the truck is still banged in from where a jitney slammed into it several years ago. They greet me with indifference, these hairy-chested men who are here to pull the net and then go back to bed. They know that I am well worth the small amount of money they pay me to get here several hours before them to do the work Tony Barbera wants done, but they are seldom in a good mood after a night of drinking, and they drink every night. I save them the trouble of getting up early or, God forbid, going to bed early.

Nine is the time to pull the net, and, since it is a real tourist attraction, many people have paid fifty cents to come and watch. I put on my oversized rubber hip boots and my rubber gloves with canvas palms and take my place in the center of the sorting pen, which is where the fish will be dumped and sorted after they are scooped up. Women, children, and men gather around me as if I were a circus announcer. I call the crowd to order and begin my speech. "Ladies and gentlemen, this is a pound net or trap net. There used to be many of these up and down the coast, but due to the scarcity of fish this is the only one left. Fish swimming up and down the coast in search of food strike the lead net, which you can see near shore. Because of fear, they then head for deep water, following the net all the way. Finally, they pass through an opening, which faces the shore, in the large net below you. Once inside they never attempt to escape by swimming toward shallow water. We will now pull the net, and I will be only too happy to answer any of your questions afterwards."

They never are really prepared for what comes up. This is a first-class appearing act. Materializing from below the water-line as we strain at the ropes threaded through the pullies are fifteen-foot sharks with their endless rows of teeth gnashing at the net, stingrays well over a hundred pounds and six feet across, flying fish, squid, stargazers, and edible fish by the ton. Back in the sorting pen, I am knee-deep in weakfish, floun-ders, kingfish, eels, rays, skates, and other fish of every size and shape.

Now my job is to identify the fish for the people who are

standing a bit farther back than they had stood moments before. Mothers are holding their children tightly, and fathers are standing protectively in front of their families. The fish market men don't like talking to the crowd, and they are anxious to get the work done, so it is up to me to pull barbs from large rays to show danger or to lift an anglerfish and show how it fishes for other fish by dangling a wormlike piece of skin in the water above its ghastly mouth; or to describe how a squid swims backward by pushing water out from an opening in its head; or how a flying fish flies by spreading its pectoral fins like wings. The large sharks present the biggest problem for the onlookers. How could these creatures exist only a short distance from where people swim? I try to reassure them that sharks are timid creatures that avoid people, but they don't really believe me. All the time I'm talking, the men are sorting the fish into crates according to need. Some boxes will go to their fish market on Arctic Avenue, some will go to local restaurants willing to pay the high price to serve the freshest fish in town, and some will go to local farmers for fertilizer. The fish market men are concerned only with crating away the fish; names mean nothing to them, but I am the namer of fish, the fixer of nets, always saddened by the thought of these magnificent rays and sharks being plowed under the ground so that Jersey tomatoes and melons will grow larger and sweeter. After the last question is answered, I help finish the sorting and the loading of the crates onto the truck even as the tourists walk back toward the boardwalk, staring at the ocean, looking for sharks.

Walking Between the Worlds

One day in late June, the Moon of Wild Strawberries, I was on an airplane flying from Chicago to Albany, New York. In that place between earth and sky, between sleep and waking, between the roar of the engines and the soft whispering of the clouds, I found myself drifting. I was sad but not afraid. I'm never afraid on airplanes, just as I never seem to have stage fright before I do a poetry reading or a story-telling performance or a lecture before an audience. Perhaps it is because I have this feeling that I'm not alone as I do these things, as I fly or speak or sing. I remember, almost a quarter of a century ago when I was teaching in West Africa, first recognizing that feeling of not being alone, of feeling a familiar and comforting presence. I could not give that presence a name then, but I can now. *Grandfather.* An old name. A presence that has grown stronger as I have grown older, as those elderly people whose lives and words have blessed me have chosen to walk to the top of that hill which rises between those who continue to breathe the winds we know and those who have chosen to go with the breath of the spirit and join their own old ones who went before them. *Grandfather.*

When I speak that word I think of the Thunders, the old strong ones whose voices we hear in the storm. Bedagiak. The Grandfathers who use their spears of lightning to destroy monsters. In 1989, when I was doing a reading in Germany, there was a sudden earth-shaking clap of thunder. "Grandfather," I said, "it is good to hear you in this land, too." Several of the people in the audience told me after the reading how much they appreciated my saying those words because it changed the whole mood. Though they'd been startled and made nervous by the thunder, my greeting to it relaxed them again. Yet I spoke those words only because they were the right words to say. *Grandfather.*

And when I speak that word I think also of the man who raised me, the Abenaki man who was my mother's father. He was quiet, even guarded about his Indian blood—though one had only to look at him to see who his ancestors were. His ways of teaching me were ways that used few if any words. One of my earliest memories is of the time I climbed the ladder with him. I do not know now if it is a true memory or if I only remember others' telling of it so well that it has become a part of me. I was only three years old. I have a picture of the two of us then. My grandfather, his face darker than a single generation of sun could make it, leans slightly to hold the left hand (the hand closest to the heart) of a very small boy with a serious face. Both the old man and the boy are looking ahead and slightly to the right, as if seeing not the camera but what is beyond it, a difficult world to walk through, a world where a child is safest when his hand is held by an elder who has been that way before.

Perhaps because of his Indian blood, perhaps just because of the way his Abenaki basketmaker parents raised him—never shouting at him, never striking him, never discouraging him from trying things that were difficult or dangerous—my grandfather was unafraid of heights. Even in his eighties he would still place the extension ladder up against the tall house and climb up to walk the peak of the roof, pausing to look toward the southeast, where the morning sun touched the edge of the hills and glittered bright as quicksilver off the lake called Saratoga.

On that day of my memory he had climbed up to look at something on the roof. Perhaps he forgot, for a moment, that

I was his shadow, always close behind him. Or perhaps he thought the rungs of the ladder too high for me to reach. But a sound made him turn and look—and see me there, at the top of the ladder, looking around, thirty feet above the ground. Another man might have shouted or grabbed at a child in such a dangerous place. But Grandfather only said, "Forgot something. Got to go back down. You go first, Sonny." And I went down the ladder, my grandfather close behind. I was a little confused when we got down, though. My grandfather didn't go get whatever it was that he had forgotten to bring up there with him. Instead he just took down the ladder and then sat there for a long time with his arm around me, not saying anything.

My mother was with me in the hospital on the day my grandfather died. It was six months after my wife and I and our year-old son had returned from Africa, come back to him and the house where I was raised, the house where I have raised my own two boys. Though sick, he'd waited for us to return, kept the house for us, tended the council fire. And now he was tired. He smiled at us—his only daughter and the child that he and his wife had taken from her to raise as his son—and said, "You go ahead and go home, I'm going to bed now."

My mother didn't understand. "But Pop," she said, "you're already in bed."

"I know where I am," Grandfather said. "I'm going to rest now. Don't you worry about me."

We left the room, and before the elevator had reached the bottom floor, his spirit had left his body. And though I cried, I knew he wasn't gone. Those who have died, my Iroquois teachers say, are no farther than the other side of a leaf that has fallen.

The late Senegalese poet Leopold Sedar Senghor wrote in one of his poems that he always confused life and death, that the two are joined by a tender bridge. It is that confusion between those two worlds, or, for Senghor's words are tinged with gentle irony, that understanding of the connection between them, that is so lacking in the lives of the majority of Americans today, including all too many of our poets. It is, I think, one of the reasons why contemporary poetry is so often a poetry of self-centeredness, of alienation, of loss and cynicism. Yet that cannot be said of most of the poetry and other writing being produced by Native American writers, by writers like myself whose lives have been deeply affected by their contacts with another way of saying and seeing the world, a gentler yet no less tough vision of reality. Those who recognize that we are always walking between the worlds which European traditions describe as "reality" and "fantasy," as "sacred" and "profane," as "natural" and "supernatural," as "life" and "death," are not immune to pain and suffering, to error and confusion; but they do tend to recognize more clearly what state, what world, they are in, and their words and their lives seek a balance which all too many others—including politicians and teachers, clergy and corporate heads—either cannot see or refuse to perceive. They cannot believe that everything around them is sacred. They cannot see the connection. But when our ears and our hearts are open, we hear things which have always been there—like the background hum of fluorescent lights in an office building or the soft drone of insects on a summer night or the wind through the grass of the prairies whispering just as the sun breaks the edge of the world and makes the shadows run across the land. As it did one June morning when my Cheyenne *nidoba* (brother-friend) Lance Henson and I stood on top of King Mountain in southwestern Oklahoma and dropped the dried needles of cedar on top of the embers of our fire so that the twenty young people, Indian and non-Indian alike, who had followed us up that mountain in the dark could wash their hands and faces—and hearts—with that cleansing ancient smoke.

When the sun was a hand's width above the horizon, we led our small group to a place that Lance and I had found the day before. It was an indentation in the stone of the mountaintop just the size of a bathtub. When we found it, it was filled with rainwater from a storm that had washed over the mountain the day before. And in that rainwater—already in that short span of time—were hundreds of tadpoles. It was such a wonderful thing to see, there on that otherwise dry mountain. We wanted to share it that dawn, to show our young writing students how quickly life can find ways to continue. But when we reached the indentation, there was no water. The dry air had sucked up that little pool. I looked at the dry stone, thinking for a moment that I might see the small, dried bodies of tadpoles. But I saw nothing. Then one of the students, Etheleen Poolaw, a Kiowa Apache girl who had struggled to come up that dark mountainside, spoke. "Look!" she said. "Look at them all." We looked where she pointed and we saw them there, and not just there but all around us. All around us, like tiny, dark stones come to life, were hundreds of small frogs, metamorphosed so quickly that some of them still had the remnants of tails. Now, as the sun rose and the mountaintop grew warmer, those small frogs were heading downslope, toward the moister, shadier places below. Continuing the cycle of their ancestors. We all watched them for a long time and then, careful where we stepped, we, too, went down the mountain.

Such moments, moments free of denial and cynicism, have helped me continue to hear my grandfather's voice and the voices of the others, old women and men who walked the circle of this land long before people imported ideas of buying and selling earth as if it were an animal to be skinned and sold and then its useless remains discarded. It was just such a moment that came to me as I sat in that plane, somewhere over central New York, the long lines of the Finger Lakes below us. It came to me as a vision of the White Dog. It was clear and real—more real, in fact, than the memory I now hold of the seat I was in and the human voices around me. For though I felt no fear as I flew in that plane, I was feeling sorrow. It was a sorrow that grows more common every day to those of us who have been taught or been given through blood that hard gift of never forgetting that our bodies and spirits and the bodies and spirits of all living things about us are connected. The thought of what was happening to life on this Earth had filled me with sadness. And then, in the place of despair, that moment came to me. I listened and sat for a time without moving. Then I said, "*Niaweh!*" (Thank you.) And I wrote in my journal these words which I offer not as a completed poem but as part of the journey:

The White Dog

After a day spent in Chicago
where a woman spoke to me
as if in a dream, tears
at the edge of her words
of how the animals all are dying,
I find myself inside an airplane.

I do not know how I have come
so far or at what actual cost
of oil surged out of wounded tundra
of smoke blackening the lungs of sky
of metals heavier than breath
slowing the blood of living waters
so that I might be part of this
rough passage of stiff wings
through razored air.

Yet, closing my eyes,
I hear the drum of Thunder

and I am in that small
darkened room at Onondaga.
Just behind that curtain
the carved basswood faces
of the Grandfathers hold
their patient knowing
gazes on that circle which was
already tomorrow yesterday.

In front of me I see the one
who has brought me here,
the White Dog I touched
ten winters ago, last of his people,
last of those who lived at Onondaga,
one of those messengers who carried
with their breaths the prayered smoke
up to Rawen Niyo's Sky Land.

Then, as now, its eyes were bright
as crystals, reflecting my face,
its stiff taxidermied limbs
holding the stance of a guardian.
It told me, Grandchild, there are ancient eyes
which measure the people, wait
for your decisions, wait for you to choose
as did the Good Mind, to help
life continue on this earth.
Even from this diminished spring
the waters can deepen,
again be sweet for those
seven generations
yet to come.

   It is sometimes hard to explain to people just what it is that
you see when you look at these worlds with something like a
native eye. Even the words you speak may seem simple and

clear but have another meaning. When you say "drum," do you see something to be played in a band or something, *some thing*, to be made by an elementary school student in a crafts class in a "Native American" unit? Or do you see a living creation, and does the word *drum*, in whatever language it is spoken, mean to you the heartbeat of Earth? When you say the word *dog*, is it a word that just means an animal or a word that is an insult? Or does it refer to one of the animal people, an honorable being, even a relative? The animals, you see, are seen as ancestors, and when native people speak of the time when animals could talk, they are speaking in the present tense. How vastly different are the views of European and Native American with regard to our animal brothers and sisters can be seen when we talk about "hunting and fishing for sport." I was in Chicago to speak on Native American publishing at the American Library Association Meeting. On the panel with me was Paul DeMain, an enrolled member of the Oneida nation, the editor of the Wisconsin native newspaper *News from Indian Country*. Much has been written recently about the opposition (violent, at times) of white sportfishing groups to the native people spearing fish, an exercise of their treaty rights (given to them in exchange for giving up the entire northern half of the state). Paul spoke of the importance of people understanding that there are different ways to see the same thing. "In our traditions," he said, "it's sacrilegious to pull a fish from the water, tear its mouth with a hook, damage the layer of protective slime on its body by taking it in your hand, and then throw it back in. To us, that is not sport. If we hunted or fished, we had good reason to do so and we did it to provide for our people. But five hundred years ago, sport in Europe was the king's army chasing a fox through the forests, while our people here on this continent were playing lacrosse and ball games which were the ancestors of football and hockey, basketball, baseball, and soccer."

The simple truth is, as Paul DeMain said, that sport to Europeans often means the killing of nonhuman beings which want no part in that sport and are given no choice, while team sports, groups of men and women playing together in agreed-upon competition, is characteristic of the native people of the Americas. The new idea of team sports (like the basic principles of democracy which the Founding Fathers borrowed from the Iroquois League) has been so wholeheartedly absorbed by white culture that there is hardly any awareness of its Native American roots. It is hard to communicate with people when they do not understand your language, though they think it is their own. And to really appreciate the writings of contemporary native people, it is also necessary to have some understanding of the living cultures that shape their thoughts and language—which is why Paul DeMain spoke of sports and fishing as part of a discussion of native publishing.

We are now in the seventh generation of native people since the coming of the Europeans five centuries ago. That period of five centuries, hard as it has been for native people, is not seen by Indians as a long time. It is still commonly said by the Iroquois and other native people that we must make our decisions not just with tomorrow's result in mind but thinking of how it will affect seven generations to come. In one of the stories of the time of Creation, there were two brothers. One was good-minded and cared for life on Earth. The other was hard-hearted, like flint. Good Mind and Flint fought each other, and when Good Mind won, the hard-hearted brother was cast out—but not out of the minds of human beings. All of us have within us those two sides. We must recognize this in order to choose the side of Good Mind, to give good thoughts strength. So, as I speak of walking between the worlds, there is also that balance to keep in mind, that balance between the human power to destroy and the human ability to preserve.

It is a difficult time to be a writer—to see a world in such incredible turmoil, to recognize how much is threatened. In some cases it turns the eyes of writers toward the decadent, toward the strange, perverse details of sex and violence to which they can connect for a momentary emotional jump-start. It is not surprising, given the devalued currency of contemporary faith and the confusion between emotional riches and material wealth that seem to be common to much of mainstream America. It is also not surprising that the other side of that coin finds some Americans looking toward the native people to find solutions. But here, too, there is often a lack of understanding. Native Americans are seen as symbols, as this decade's equivalent of the Maharishi or Bagwan Rajneesh. Like Columbus, some Americans get their Indians mixed up.

Trying to fill the emptiness in your heart, the hole in the American soul, with Indians, especially Indians seen as "mystic warriors" or "noble savages," no more real than the image on the old buffalo nickel, is both an exercise in self-deception and yet another form of racism. Understanding Native Americans does not mean becoming Indian. Understanding Native Americans begins with non-Indians understanding themselves. It is my belief—or at least my hope—that all human beings have that ability to walk between the worlds in their own ways. People who have worked hard on the kind of courageous self-awareness that characterizes ACOA and Alcoholics Anonymous programs do not become cynical or discouraged; they find within themselves spiritual depths they had not known existed—or had deliberately avoided acknowledging. In acknowledging a Higher Power, they are ready to acknowledge the workings of something greater than themselves in the world and the people around them.

It was dark when the plane landed in Albany and I walked toward my car in the lot. I looked, I am sure, no different from many others leaving that same airport. Few would notice the bear claw I wear around my neck or see the sweetgrass braid on the car's dashboard. Perhaps no others leaving that airport would speak a few words of thanks and greeting to the wide Mohawk River as they crossed over it. But though I share the words of my poems—and this essay—with anyone who has the patience to read them, I do not carry that bear claw and that sweetgrass just so that others can see them, and though I have much to be thankful for, I usually say my prayers of thanksgiving quietly. Indeed, as I started the engine and turned the wheel toward the north and the house where my grandfather raised me, I knew that many things which others did not see were carrying me, helping me to stay in balance, guiding me like my grandfather's voice. As I followed the light cast by my own passage along the dark road I gave thanks for the gift of yet another day of walking between the worlds.

Beyond the Crust

I am very fond of bread. I am an extremely adventurous eater and will try any dish from any ethnic cuisine, and nine times out of ten I will enjoy the food and try it again. Open as I am to new food, though, when I approach bread I become the obverse of myself. Instead of the easygoing Puerto Rican that I think I am, I become gravely suspicious when I approach bread— it must prove itself to me. Bread is an elixer that can turn me into a Ferdinand the Bull, content and dreamy, or bring out the fierce Mr. Hyde in me.

It's not that I want fancy breads or pastries. I've had memorable breakfasts that consisted only of coffee and milk, bread and butter—the daily and traditional breakfast of many people in Puerto Rico, especially in the generations before mine. They went to their local baker and got a piece of bread cut from a whole loaf. A penny bought a piece of bread and a wipe of butter. (*Un chavo de pan unta'o.*) With a pot of fresh coffee and, if you could afford it, a side of condensed milk, you started the day, prepared to face the world.

I have often wondered about the origins of such a breakfast. Was it ethnic or economic? What else could poor people eat for breakfast? Or did poor people in their wisdom know that such a breakfast was the best way to start a day? When I went to Europe and faced my first so-called continental breakfast, it turned out to be *un chavo de pan* with a very fancy *unta'o*. The base of the breakfast was the same, but the pastry and preserves, jams and jellies, made me wonder if money takes us away from our collective wisdom, leading us to overdoses of sugar.

When traveling or away from home for a long period, the food I most long for and urgently miss is my favorite loaf of bread—either with butter and coffee or securely enclosing cold cuts like mortadella or Genoa salami. Nothing seems to me more satisfying than a loaf of Italian bread, hard and crusty but not flaky, baked a rich brown (the color of my skin), sprinkled with sesame seeds, stuffed with quality tuna fish swimming in Hellman's mayonnaise, blanketed with rings of ripe plum tomatoes, and with a side dish of radishes and spears of cucumber or quarters of deep green, red, or yellow bell peppers. Accompanied by a glass of wine, a cold beer, even a soda or a glass of milk, I say no man ever ate better. When my teeth crash through the crust and I get the first rush of blended tastes, I say, "Hallelujah, the hero sandwich. Thank you Italians for coming to America."

Fink Means Good Bread said the sides of the white van that parked regularly on the northbound side of Lexington Avenue in Spanish Harlem in 1945. From the window of my fifth-floor apartment across the street I watched the driver–delivery man carry his white-wrapped, long, square loaves of Fink bread into the Jewish delicatessen. On the window was written 7W2 in Hebrew letters. At least, that's what they looked like to me and how I read them.

Though only across the avenue from me, the 7W2 delicatessen was outside my world. What they sold, and to whom, was beyond me. My parents never went out to restaurants and never brought home cooked food from anywhere in those days. Although the deli was the nearest restaurant to our apartment building, I didn't know rye, nor pastrami. Corned beef was something that came out of a Libby can, and my mother served it with white rice and peas; a very pleasing combination, and quick to prepare—important qualities for a woman who worked all day as a seamstress and then came home to cook.

I had a very good friend in grammar school named Selwyn

Kessler. We talked about many things—including what the Germans were doing to the Jews and how his cousin had changed his name to Kess in order to avoid discrimination at the American medical school he wanted to attend. It was the first I had heard of prejudice against Jews. I had thought that prejudice meant discrimination against Puerto Ricans. To me, Selwyn looked like an American, and I couldn't figure out why anybody would not want him in a college, let alone try to exterminate him. Selwyn made me think it wasn't so bad to be Puerto Rican, even though we definitely did not look American.

Selwyn Kessler took me to his father's ice cream parlor on Madison Avenue between 108th and 109th streets in east Harlem. In the back of the store Selwyn had built a simple darkroom from plans in an issue of *Popular Mechanics*. But all I had to eat was a scoop of very good peach-flavored ice cream in a wafer cone. This was Jewish food?

Selwyn Kessler, why didn't you ever talk to me about pastrami, rye bread, or bagels? Especially bagels! It took a Cuban Jew who worked the night shift with me in the main post office in Manhattan to introduce me to bagels and lox, a combination that is high on my list of robust tastes, and which I go after frequently. Selwyn, I could have been such a happy kid with a breakfast of bagels instead of oatmeal or farina! Why did we talk only about politics?

My parents had a charge account at the local Puerto Rican grocery store, Dulfo's Bodega—Dulfo short for Rodulfo. The charge account was easy to administer, and there were no plastic cards or forms to fill out, no bills in the mail, and no copying your driver's license number ad nauseum. Whenever I went to the store to get a P&G bread, I would say, "Put it in our book, Dulfo," and Dulfo would take out a book, turn to the page with my parents' name on it, and enter the amount for the loaf of bread. This system was terrific and everyone used it—and as

I think about our working-class status, it was probably indispensable. But as I was never given money to buy it, I can't say what I paid for a loaf of unsliced P&G bread. Nor do I know who baked it or what P&G stood for.

P&G was good. It was soft-crunchy, baked to a light color, and had only a few sesame seeds. It was basically white bread shaped like an Italian loaf; it came unwrapped, and Dulfo put it in a brown paper bag. If I was charging several items, that same bag was used for calculations. And one of the greater sights of the store was to watch Dulfo rapidly add up a column of forty or so entries on the paper bag. You stayed out of the store on Saturdays because everyone was in there, shopping and settling bills, and frequently there were disputes. Was Dulfo padding the accounts? I don't know, but after a time, I went to the store with my own little book, and Dulfo entered the amount in my book *and* in his book.

I think that today I would classify P&G with the kind of inferior breads I see by the door at my local supermarket. P&G was modeled after the real McCoy, but any resemblance was purely imaginary. Must all ethnic products move into an amorphous center—a center where Italian bread is neither Italian nor American but something else, not as good as either? Something like me—not quite all Puerto Rican, not quite all American. Am I like bread because of this process, in danger of moving to an insipid center? No! I know I am rich and better for incorporating more cultures, but the bread didn't incorporate—it diluted, trying to please everyone. Today I see something in the supermarkets that I call Son of P&G; it comes in its own printed bag, which usually says Italian Bread. It is a bread that Mr. Hyde won't let me buy or eat, and the rational Mr. Agüeros finds pathetic to the eye and palate—a bread for feeding to pigeons.

We alternated our usual P&G with Silvercup. Silvercup was white sliced bread, nicely packaged, so soft that if you care-

lessly put it in a bag with cans leaning on it, it would be de-
formed by the time you got home. It was American Bread,
wherever that came from. It was a bread that tasted like nothing, moved into tastelessness because of the needs or desires
of mass production and profit-making. Somewhere in the uni-
verse, as in Plato's theory, there is an archetypal white bread
that perhaps existed in America when people made their own
bread at home. But today's version is a tasteless descendant;
no wonder the phrase "like white bread" is pejorative.

White bread is to bread what the Red Delicious apple is to
apples or the Barbie doll is to women.

We kept our bread in a tin box, where it seemed to stay
fresh for long periods. I have never understood why the bread
box worked, but when the bread finally became stale, it wasn't
thrown out. When there was enough old bread my father made
a delicious bread pudding, soaking the old bread in milk and
adding vanilla flavoring and raisins. When it was baking, the
aroma overpowered the whole apartment. If there was too
much bread, or moldy pieces, my father would kiss each piece
and say, "May God forgive me" as he tossed the pieces into
the garbage can. I understood that throwing away bread was a
very serious act.

It was hard to forget the importance of bread. Right over the
main door to our apartment there was a framed picture of the
Virgin Dolorosa, and tied to the frame there was a horseshoe,
a sprig of palm leaf folded into a cross, and a hunk of dried
bread. Each item had its talismanic purpose, especially con-
fusing to me as my parents were neither religious nor supersti-
tious.

My mother would say "longer than a day without bread," in
Spanish, when she wanted to make a point about how awful
something was, such as a double header on television or a
lengthy and cramped ride in the family car.

On Sundays my father would go off for special bread baked

on Park Avenue around 114th Street. There, at a bakery perhaps German, perhaps Jewish, perhaps both, he bought what I now call kaiser rolls—soft-crusted rolls sprinkled with black poppy seeds. My mother would have been up late the night before deep-frying chicken in a big, deep, black iron pot. That chicken, now cold, would go into the rolls as fried chicken sandwiches. Although it was only seven or eight in the morning, I already wanted one, but I waited until noon or so, when we would be on a beach—maybe South Beach on Staten Island, maybe Jones Beach on Long Island, maybe Orchard Beach in the Bronx. I never knew where I was going, and my father seemed to decide just as we were leaving the house.

Whatever beach we were on, I was satisfied and secure in the knowledge that no one else on the beach had sandwiches as good as ours. Periodically it happens that I have a flashback to those days, and my mouth waters and my eyes tear because I have no distinguished multicultural sandwich of Puerto Rican fried chicken on a kaiser roll. This hunger and nostalgia has overtaken me in odd places at odd times, and I have never learned a satisfactory way to deal with it—certainly, trying to substitute something tasty absolutely does not work. When that latent image of the desirable bread rises up in my mind's eye, nothing but the real product can satisfy the call, because I am beyond the crust.

My friend Roland Cintron was and is mad about bread. He had a favorite bakery on 3d Avenue up around 103d Street. I don't remember what ethnicity the owners were. I would walk him there sometimes on Sunday after mass, and he would buy two loaves. But by the time he got back to 109th Street and Lexington a good half of one loaf would be gone. This always shocked me, because in my family there was only one rule about bread, but it was a solemn rule. *Do not pick at the bread or eat the teat on the way home.* (The teat is what we called the ends of the pointy loaf. I loved the teats and always got them at home; they were the crunchiest and best-cooked part of the loaf.)

Obviously Roland had no such rule because he would say to me, "Put this piece in your mouth and chew it a little but don't swallow it right away. Saliva in the mouth acts upon the dough and converts it into sugar. Ummmm." So I would take a little wad of the inner core and chew it slowly. But it never happened for me—it never tasted like sugar. When Roland got home he would take a bottle of milk and sit down with the balance of his picked-on loaf and wash the bread down with milk and then wash the milk down with bread. The other loaf I guess was shared by the rest of the family.

Another friend, Angelo, introduced me to the avocado sandwich, with the skin and all. Taking a Sicilian loaf, he would remove the insides, cut up the avocado into wide slices, lay them in the bread, salt them, and plop the top over them. I hope the skin gave us roughage, because avocado sandwiches were more delicious without the skins, but how could I say that to Angelo?

My mother said that there was nothing better than a piece of crusty Italian bread and a banana. Not as a sandwich, but just together. When my mother ate white bread, she neatly cut all around the perimeter of the slice, removing the crust. With Italian bread she removed the inside, as I do. (In Spanish we call this inside the *tripa*, the "intestine" of the bread.) I would tease her about this seeming contradiction, but inwardly I knew that it was not a contradiction, because store-bought white bread deserves a vocabulary of its own, and to speak of crust on this bread as if it were the same thing as on a real loaf of bread is to abuse the language.

Of all my childhood friends, I'll always remember Tommy Barbieri. Tommy is Italian, and I met him in Benjamin Franklin High School, which was in the Italian section of East Harlem. So on my way to high school I would first stop and ring

Joey Campisi's bell on 3d Avenue, and then together we would go around the corner on 115th Street between 3d and 2d and call Tommy down from one of the many brownstones that lined the south side of the street then.

By the time I was a teenager there was no bread but Italian bread for me. One day Tommy Barbieri had brought me down a piece of a round loaf of bread cut into halves along its equator, sprinkled with olive oil and garlic, and heated in the oven. As a Puerto Rican I was used to olive oil and garlic, but the bread that Tommy gave me was far superior to the P&G I was used to. My teeth had to work to get through the crust, and I felt like a primitive man ripping into something like the hide of a mastodon—tough and gamy, then hitting the sublime oil and garlic.

My face still contorts when I remember the time I ate the most disgusting bread ever. Roland had invited me to Central Park, where the army was putting on something called the War Show or the War Games. I suppose it was part of morale building on the home front, or maybe they were showing off just after winning the war. We wandered over to the great lawn around Belvedere Lake and Castle, where today the Delacorte Theatre stands. At the show we saw parades of military costumes for different battle zones and terrains. A most impressive display of a weapon called a "flame thrower" was put on, with great sheets of fire snapping out over the lake, searing the grass on the shore's edge. Around the perimeter of the lawn, the army had tents displaying various war matériel, and at one of the tents a soldier was passing out samples of a bread he claimed the Germans were synthesizing from sawdust, a black, heavy bread. We were given a small sample to try. Both Roland and I took a bite and quickly spit it out. Not too much synthesizing as far as I was concerned, and if Selwyn had made me mad at the Germans already, eating sawdust gave me another reason to dislike them.

I first tried French bread in New York. I liked the way it looked, but the thinness of the baguette makes it hard to qualify as a good bread for the sort of sandwich that I consider essential to life. In France I found the bread tastier, very good with butter, and even fairly good around the ham sandwich that the French serve in their cafés. Back in New York I buy a French loaf only now and then; they never seem as tasty and crisp, and I miss the original.

Today I have two favorite bakeries in New York. My most favorite I worry about because of the real estate pressures of Manhattan. The Palermo Bakery sits on First Avenue and makes the most magnificent breads and bread sticks in the world. Every time I go there I suffer a little because I fear that one day it will be gone, replaced by some dippy yuppie store. It has happened to me with other favorite bakeries.

Not only does Palermo have truly great breads, but the baker is an artist, making loaves he calls "fishes" and "twists," small loaves he calls "footballs," round loaves in two sizes, and bread sticks covered in sesame seeds. Each loaf is an artifact—an example of decorative art—to be displayed on the table as proudly as blown glass or antique silverware. My body is fed twice: my eyes feast, my stomach feasts.

My second favorite baker is closer to my apartment and seems more secure. Zito's in the Village is a bread store that started around the turn of the century and bakes two or three times a day; if you time your visit right, you can get hot whole wheat, regular, or semolina bread in long loaves, twists, or rounds. Zito's seems more permanent and more likely to remain, as the neighborhood around it is still full of Italian shops and an Italian population. But the texture and taste, while very good, do not equal Palermo's quality in my mouth.

But will Zito's heirs want to bake bread and stay in the city? Or will his kids study medicine and business and move out to the 'burbs and gradually shift to white bread because driving down to where you get good bread is too much trouble, and anyway the kids like white bread because they see it on television?

I shudder. America, your ethnicity is your strength! Italian bread—get on television! You build bodies ELEVEN ways, making my eyes roll and strengthening my jaw muscles as I bite, rattling my tympanum as I pulverize that crust and chop the cold cuts—plus the other eight good ingredients in the wheat!

But here I am bemoaning the possible flight from ethnic heritage of the Italians, and I haven't even once mentioned Puerto Rican bread! Why haven't I? Have I lost my roots crossing over to Italian bread? No!

At the time I was growing up, the Puerto Ricans did not have many bakeries in New York. The few that existed seemed to be more interested in baking birthday and wedding cakes, and the most famous chain in New York, Valencia Bakeries, still specializes in occasion cakes. My father either couldn't get any or there was no Puerto Rican bread to be had in the neighborhood.

Puerto Ricans favor a bread made with water (*pan de agua*) and one made with lard (*pan de manteca*). Both are baked only lightly, and they have a very soft crust, which is also flaky. They do not lend themselves to making robust sandwiches. They are very tasty with butter and coffee, and excellent for mopping up sauces. I do not live within walking distance of a Puerto Rican bakery, but periodically I travel to neighborhoods where the Puerto Ricans, the Cubans, and the Dominicans all make a very similar bread. The Cuban sandwich has taken hold in New York and is crossing over to New Yorkers generally. This is partly due to the fact that in grilling, the bread picks up the lateral strength necessary to hold the hams, cheese, and pickle inside. If the bread wasn't grilled, it would fall apart at the first bite, and no one likes a crumbly sandwich.

It wasn't until recently, though, that I first tasted the best bread I have eaten in Puerto Rico—a bread that immediately went very high up on my list of excellent breads.

My mother had moved just outside the town of Quebradillas, the place of her birth. She heard about a man who baked bread the old-fashioned way, in a wood-burning oven. I immediately jumped in a car and drove to the place, nearly missing it, as it didn't even have a sign.

Inside the shop I felt I had returned to a past era. No decoration whatsoever, only function. The shop had an aroma of burning wood blended with an aroma of bread which made my mouth water. The loaves were sold by weight—"Do you want a pound loaf?" I answered yes before inquiring what other weight there was, then asked for another when the pound looked like the regular size. The bread had a beautiful yellow-orange color to it, and nestled in the center was a bit of palm leaf. It was simple and beautiful, the palm leaf an attractive, unexpected, and understated, but dramatic, touch. And for once I regretted that the store was not crowded, for I wanted to stand and make mental notes of the locale and its atmosphere. Leave it to the tourist to want to stand and gawk while the natives rush in and out, anxious to be somewhere else. In the car, I could not keep the solemn rule. I broke off the teat and started eating it as I drove. It was as wonderful as it smelled and looked.

Plain, I chewed it and thought of Roland, but it still didn't taste sweet. At home, I asked my mother why the baker put a piece of palm leaf on each loaf.

"That's his secret. He says it gives the bread a special taste. And the yellow-orange color is due to his use of fresh egg yolks from chickens who walk free."

A superb bread, but three and a half hours away by jet.

Ah, Bread, you make me realize that it is hard and wasteful to be purely ethnic in America—definitely wasteful to be totally assimilated.

Contributors

Kathleen Aguero is the author of two collections of poetry: *Thirsty Day* (Alice James Books, 1977) and *The Real Weather* (Hanging Loose Press, 1987). With Marie Harris, she edited *A Gift of Tongues: Critical Challenges in Contemporary American Poetry* (University of Georgia Press, 1987) and *An Ear to the Ground: An Anthology of Contemporary American Poetry* (University of Georgia Press, 1989). She teaches at Pine Manor College in Chestnut Hill, Massachusetts.

Jack Agüeros was born in East Harlem to Puerto Rican parents. He is a published poet, essayist, and short story writer who has also written for television and radio. Mr. Agüeros directed El Museo del Barrio, the only Puerto Rican museum in the United States, for nearly ten years and is one of the cofounders of the Festival Latino in New York and a member of the Professional Playwright's unit at the Puerto Rican Traveling Theatre's Playwrights. His play, *The News from Puerto Rico*, won first prize in the 1989 McDonald's Latino Dramatists' Competition, and his first book of poetry, *Correspondence Between the Stonehaulers*, was published by Hanging Loose Press in 1991.

Joseph Bruchac, of Slovak, Abenaki, and English ancestry, writes poetry, fiction, and literary criticism. He is the author of numerous books of poetry and fiction, including the poetry collection *Near the Mountains* (White Pine Press, 1987). He has also published three collections of retellings of Iroquois folk stories and a collection of interviews with American Indian poets, *Survival Comes This Way* (University of Arizona Press, 1987). He has been instrumental in starting writing workshops in American prisons, and, with his wife, Carol, he founded the Greenfield Review Press. He has edited ten anthologies, including *Songs from This Earth on Turtle's Back* (Greenfield Review Press, 1983); *The Light from Another Country* (Greenfield Review

Press, 1984), a collection of poetry from Americans in prison; and the award-winning *Breaking Silence: An Anthology of Contemporary Asian American Poets* (Greenfield Review Press, 1983).

Judith Ortiz Cofer is a native of Puerto Rico now living in Georgia with her family. She is the author of *The Line of the Sun* (University of Georgia Press, 1989); two poetry collections: *Terms of Survival* (Arte Publico Press, 1987) and *Reaching for the Mainland* (Bilingual Press, 1987); and a collection of personal essays and poems: *Silent Dancing: A Partial Remembrance of a Puerto Rican Childhood* (Arte Publico Press, 1990), which received a PEN American/Albrand Special Citation. She has received fellowships from the National Endowment for the Arts, the Witter Bynner Foundation for Poetry, and the Bread Loaf Writers' Conference, among others.

Sam Cornish lives in Boston and teaches at Emerson College. He has published three books of poems, including *Songs of Jubilee: New and Selected Poems* (Unicorn Press, 1986). His book reviews appear in the *Christian Science Monitor* and other periodicals. *1935: A Memoir* is his most recent work (Ploughshares Books, 1991).

Kiana Davenport, of Hawaiian and Dutch descent, is the author of three novels: *Wild Spenders* (Macmillan, 1984), *The Power Eaters* (William Morrow, 1980), and *A Desperate Season* (Fawcett, 1979). She is completing a collection of stories, *Pacific Woman*, about women of Pacific island-nations emerging in the modern age. She is the recipient of fiction grants from the Ingram Merrill Foundation, the New York Foundation for the Arts, Money for Women/Barbara Deming Memorial Fund, and the Ludwig Vogelstein Foundation. She has also received a 1992 NEA Fiction Fellowship and a Bunting Fiction Fellowship at Radcliffe for 1992–93.

Toi Derricotte has published three collections of poetry, most recently *Captivity* (University of Pittsburgh Press, 1989). Her previous collections are *Natural Birth* (Crossing Press, 1983) and *The Empress of the Death House* (Lotus Press, 1978). She is the recipient of two fellowships from the National Endowment for the Arts. She is associate professor of English at the University of Pittsburgh.

Richard Hoffman was born in Allentown, Pennsylvania, in 1949. A poet, essayist, and fiction writer, his work has appeared in *Hudson Review*, *Kansas Quarterly*, *Shenandoah*, and the *Sun*, as well as in several anthologies, including *An Ear to the Ground* (University of Georgia Press, 1989). He has received fellowships from the New Jersey Council on the Arts and the Massachusetts Artists' Foundation. His essay in this volume is an excerpt from a work in progress, *Pennsylvania Power & Light: A Memoir*.

Garrett Hongo, a poet, is associate professor of English and Director of Creative Writing at the University of Oregon. His honors include the Lamont Poetry Prize, the Discovery/*The Nation* Prize, and two fellowships from the National Endowment for the Arts. He is currently a Guggenheim Fellow. His books are *Yellow Light* (Wesleyan, 1982) and *The River of Heaven* (Knopf, 1988). He returns regularly to his home village in Hawaii, where he is writing a memoir entitled *Volcano Journal*.

Norman Paul Hyett spent his childhood in Atlantic City, New Jersey. He is a psychologist and guidance counselor. Married, with two children, he lives in Brookline, Massachusetts.

Lonny Kaneko is a sansei poet whose chapbook *Coming Home from Camp* (Brooding Heron Press, 1986) reflects his family's experiences during and after their World War II internment in Minidoka, Idaho. His work appears in anthologies, including *Breaking Silence* (Greenfield Review Press, 1983), *Ayumi* (Japanese American Anthology Committee, 1980), and *An Ear to the Ground* (University of Georgia Press, 1989). He has received a fellowship from the National Endowment for the Arts and is coauthor, with Amy Sanbo, of two plays.

Suzanne Odette Khuri left Lebanon as a child and visited for the last time in the summer of 1975. Since graduating from Radcliffe College in 1978 she has worked extensively as a writer, director, performer, and teacher in Europe and North America. She cowrote and performed *This Is for You, Anna*, which toured throughout Canada and England, winning several awards. Her creation *How Many Ways*

Can You Sit in a Chair? is a solo show based on diaries kept by women in Beirut, Lebanon. She also cofounded Ad Astra Productions. She lives in Brooklyn, New York.

Leslie Lawrence is a recipient of fellowships from the Massachusetts Artists' Foundation and the National Endowment for the Arts. Her stories have appeared in the anthologies *Feeding the Hungry Heart* (Bobbs-Merrill, 1982) and *Women on Women* (Plume, 1990), and in the *Massachusetts Review*, the *Colorado Review*, and others. She lives in Cambridge, Massachusetts.

Robert Peters, although best known as a poet, is also an actor, playwright, and critic whose books include *Selected and New Poems: 1967–1990* (Asylum Press, 1992), and *Snapshots for a Serial Killer: A Fiction and a Play* (GLB Publishers, 1992). His essay "Brother" is a continuation of his ongoing memoirs, the earliest being his much-acclaimed *Crunching Gravel: On Growing up in the Thirties* (Mercury House, 1988). Among his numerous awards are a Guggenheim Fellowship, a National Endowment for the Arts Fellowship, and the de Castagnola Prize from the Poetry Society of America.

Minnie Bruce Pratt has published three volumes of poetry: *The Sound of One Fork* (Night Heron Press, 1981), *We Say We Love Each Other* (Spinsters Aunt Lute, 1985), and *Crime Against Nature* (Firebrand Books, 1990), which was the winner of the 1989 Lamont Poetry Prize. She has received a National Endowment for the Arts Fellowship and in 1991 was a recipient of the Lillian Hellman–Dashiell Hammett Award given by the Fund for Free Expression to writers "victimized by political persecution." She has also completed a book of autobiographical essays, *Rebellion: Essays 1980–1991* (Firebrand Books, 1991).

Alberto Alvaro Ríos is a professor of English at Arizona State University. He has published eight books of poetry, the most recent being *Teodoro Luna's Two Kisses* (Norton, 1990), and his work has appeared in numerous journals and poetry anthologies, including *The Norton Anthology of Modern Poetry* (1988) and *The Morrow Anthology of Younger American Poets* (1985). He has also published fiction and received many awards and fellowships, including a Guggenheim Fellowship in poetry, the Western States Book Award for Fiction, the Walt Whitman Award, and a National Endowment for the Arts Award in poetry.

Gary Soto has written several poetry and prose collections, including *Pacific Crossing* (Harcourt Brace Jovanovich, 1992), *The Elements of San Joaquin* (University of Pittsburgh Press, 1977), *Living Up the Street* (Strawberry Hill, 1985) (for which he received a Before Columbus Foundation 1985 American Book Award), *A Summer Life* (University Press of New England, 1990), *Baseball in April* (Harbrace, 1990), and *Who Will Know Us?* (Chronicle Books, 1990). He has received an Academy of American Poets Prize, the Discovery/*The Nation* Prize, and the U.S. Award of the International Poetry Forum, in addition to fellowships from the Guggenheim Foundation, the National Endowment for the Arts, and the California Arts Council. He has produced two films for Mexican American children. He lives with his wife and daughter in Berkeley, California.

Yvonne is a poet and filmmaker. A former poetry editor at *Ms.* magazine and at *Aphra*, she is the author of a three-volume epic, *The Iwilla Trilogy* (Chameleon Productions, 1985, 1986, 1990). A graduate of Rosemont College, a Catholic women's college in Pennsylvania, she is at work on a book of essays on Black Catholicism and a collection of short fiction. In 1991 she won the BRIO Award for poetry.